SHameLeSS
SELF PROMOTION

For His Glory!

Paula K Parker

SHAMELESS
SELF PROMOTION

PAULA K. PARKER, MIKE PARKER & TORRY MARTIN

WordCrafts

.

Shameless Self Promotion
 and Networking for Christian Creatives
Copyright © 2011
Paula K. Parker, Mike Parker, Torry Martin

Cover art & design by Kevin Tucker & Ben Harper for Collide Creative
Author photos by Allen Clark

Published by WordCrafts Press
Tullahoma, TN 37388
www.wordcrafts.net

CONTENTS

*Do nothing out of selfish ambition or vain conceit;
but in humility consider others better than yourself!*

Prologue

This is a prologue.

Yes, we know; most people see the word, **Prologue**, and flip past it to get to the real book, thinking that the prologue is an archaic and boring addition to the beginning of a book and about as useful as lips on a chicken; and after all, who wants to kiss a chicken?

But, trust us; there is a reason for this prologue. We mean, honestly, every great book begins with a prologue and who are we to challenge the system?

"Indeed," you ask, "just who *are* you to be writing a book on shameless self promotion... much less one with a prologue?"

Ah, a challenge. You want to know our credentials? Very

astute question. Let's see if our answer is equally astute.

Our Credentials

The three authors of this book have a combined 55 years - yes, we *are* that old - of professional experience working in various segments of the Christian and general market entertainment industries.

Mike and Paula K. Parker

Since 1995 the husband and wife writing team of Mike and Paula K. Parker have interviewed hundreds, nay thousands, of people from all walks of life - from superstar actors like Orlando Bloom, Pierce Brosnan, Harry Connick, Jr., Danny DeVito, Colin Firth, Morgan Freeman, Laura Linney, James Marsden, Emma Thompson, Rachel Weiss and Michael York; to Oscar-winning directors like Jerry Bruckheimer, Peter Jackson, and Sir Ridley Scott. They've talked to Grammy Award-winning recording artists like Jars of Clay, LL Cool J, Steven Curtis Chapman, and Michael W. Smith; guitar legends like Phil Keaggy and Gordon Kennedy; sensitive singer/songwriter-types like Margaret Becker, Annie Herring, and Andrew Peterson; world-class composers like Howard Shore (Lord of the Rings Trilogy) and Harry Gregson-Williams (Kingdom of Heaven, The Chronicles of Narnia: The Lion, The Witch and the Wardrobe); and best-selling authors like Douglas Gresham, Frank Peretti, Nicholas Sparks, and GP Taylor. [We could go on and on, but that would just be pretentious.]

They've also interviewed experts in countless career fields and endeavors, from runway models to Olympic athletes, cave explorers to infertility specialists, from theologians to shoe salesmen, from homemakers and educators to politicians and public health officials. Their works, collectively and individually, have been published in dozens of national periodicals and prominent online websites. Their books include both fiction and non-fiction and their stage plays have been performed by theatrical companies across the United States.

Torry Martin

Torry Martin is an award-winning actor, screenwriter, comedian and author. In addition to penning humor columns for a variety of national print and online publications including Cloud Ten Pictures, On Course Magazine, Enrichment Journal, Front Yard Worship and Clubhouse Magazine, Martin is the author of seven comedy sketchbooks published by Lillenas Drama Publishers. Torry's unique sense of humor caught the attention of the producers of the popular children's radio series, "Adventures in Odyssey," who enlisted him to lend his writing skills to the show. Martin went one step further, creating the delightful recurring character of Wooton Bassett, based loosely on himself.

An accomplished actor, Torry starred in the national touring company of Columbia Artist's musical comedy, "Around the World in Eighty Days." He has appeared on The Learning Channel and the Fine Living Network; won top honors as both writer and actor in the Nashville 48 Hour Film Project; and has twice been named Grand Prize Winner for both Acting and Writing by the Gospel Music Association. A storyteller at heart, Torry has graced the stages of hundreds of secular and sacred venues across the country, sharing a brand of comedy described by author Paul McCusker as, "Garrison Keillor with a spiritual perspective."

Torry has developed a unique approach to networking that

eschews the common idea of *'what can you do for me,'* and turns it around with a *'how can I help you?'* attitude. As Rene Gutteridge, popular screenwriter and author of 16 novels said, "When you meet Torry Martin, you suddenly have 300 new friends."

Combined…

We've had the privilege to work with some of the top editors, influential writers, publicists, copy editors, and PR experts in the industry, many of whom we count as friends.

One thing we've learned - everybody has a story. Another thing we've learned - not everyone knows how to tell their story well. It pains us to see people without the tools to promote their message or product, or watch them stumble through an interview, little realizing how they appear to their audience or how it affects the article that will be written about them.

Creative people are often right-brain dominant; but while the right-brain opens the door, it's usually the left-brain that does the business. That is why we wrote this book. *Shameless Self Promotion and Networking for Christian Creatives* is designed to help equip you, whether you are an individual or an organization, with the tools you need for successful self-promotion, using tried and proven methods and without the need to sell your soul in the process.

Who would benefit by this book?

- Actors
- Artists
- Authors
- Church leaders
- Event organizers

- Filmmakers
- Musicians
- Photographers
- Painters
- Sculptors
- Speakers

...and just about anybody else with a story to tell; which is just about everybody else.

It is not our intent to limit the people who fit into this group. If you have a unique talent that doesn't fit this list, but still needs promotion, this book is for you. Perhaps you are not in *"The Christian Entertainment Industry."* Perhaps you are an ordinary person caught up in extraordinary circumstances. Perhaps you are an expert in your field. Perhaps you are a church, school, or business that has need of publicity for an event. For whatever reason, you have a story to tell and you've been given the platform to tell it. It is your obligation to tell it well. This book will help you do that.

Indie and Signed

If you are an independent artist, you already know that the burden of promotion rests upon your shoulders. If you're a signed artist/author/actor, chances are the promotions ball is still in your court. The old days of, "I signed a contract and all I have to do is sit back and let the royalties roll in," are gone. In fact, we doubt they ever existed. Today, even signed artists with an established track record must be heavily involved in promoting their own work if they want to continue to succeed. Just ask NY Times best-selling author, GP Taylor.

In 2004, while still a vicar with the Church of England – he has since retired – he sold his motorcycle to raise the money to self-publish his first novel, the Young Adult supernatural thriller, "Shadowmancer." Acting as his own publicist, Taylor gathered a list of media outlets and began contacting them with press releases he wrote himself. "Shadowmancer" was an instant smash hit. Taylor was later approached by one of the UK's largest publishing houses, leading to multi-book contracts, movie rights and international notoriety. "Shadowmancer" went on to become a New York Times best-selling novel.

Taylor has since written nine more novels utilizing the services of traditional publishing houses. Although these companies either have their own publicity departments, or outsource publicity to independent firms, Taylor has never stopped shamelessly self promoting his books.

"Who knows a book better - or wants to see it succeed more - than the author?" Taylor asks. "I continue to add to my list of media outlets and regularly send out press releases with news that relate to my books or their message."

What You Will Find in This Book

Shameless Self Promotion and Networking for Christian Creatives is divided into six chapters.

In **Chapter One**, we look at you and what you are trying to promote - whether it is a book, a CD, an upcoming concert tour, an event at your church, or your own personal ministry.

Chapter Two discusses your press kit and tells you, in the words of Bob Seeger, *"What to leave, what to leave out."* A fresh press kit is a good press kit. We'll tell you how to keep it fresh.

Chapter Three covers publicity and how to promote yourself, your project and your message without selling your soul for 15 minutes of fame.

Chapter Four deals with that gut-wrenching, nail-biting, break-out-in-hives-and-cold-sweats event known as *The Interview.* [It can be intimidating, but you can do it; we *know* you can.] This section includes helpful hints for pre-interview preparation, the interview, and the post-interview follow-up and evaluation.

Chapter Five explains how to effectively brand and market yourself and your products.

Chapter Six looks at networking from a Christian perspective.

In each section, we will include anecdotal examples of good shameless self promotion, and maybe some cringe-worthy examples of shameful self promotion to avoid.

I Think I Can, I Think I Can

Now that you know what this book is about, you might wonder, *Can I do this? Do I have what it takes to promote my book/CD/film/show/myself?*

Yes, you can - and yes, you do!

Paula, Mike and Torry all began as independent artists. We all learned - through trial and error and with lots of advice from industry experts - what worked and what didn't.

"I started off on 80 acres in Bear Valley, Alaska," Torry notes. "Not exactly the Entertainment Capital of the World. But people invested in me and I want to turn around and do the same for other people who are living in their own little cabin, wherever they are, to help them get their message heard. If someone from the mountains of Alaska can do this, anybody can."

This book will help you write your own success story, rather than waiting for someone else to write it for you.

Butcher, Baker, Candlestick Maker

Since this book is written for creative people in all fields, it would be awkward – not to mention time-consuming – to list all the different artistic fields each time we referred to a person or project. Throughout the book, we will use the different artistic titles – author, actor, singer, painter, etc. – and the different creative fields/projects – books, CDs, concerts, portraits, etc. – interchangeably. It is not our intention to favor one over the other. If something speaks uniquely to a specific person, project, skill or artistic endeavor we will mention it. Otherwise, figure it all applies to you.

It's a Team Effort

If you have a signed contract with an entertainment-oriented company, such as a record label or book publisher, then you have a team who has a stake in helping you promote your work. Depending upon the details of your particular situation, that team might include:

- A Manager
- A Booking Agent

- A Publicist
- An A&R Executive
- A Publisher
- An Editor
- A Graphic Designer
- A Marketing Team
- A Host of Other Professionals

...and of course, never underestimate the power of a pushy stage mother.

These people have the experience and expertise to promote you and your book/CD/film to the appropriate journalists and media outlets. If you are smart – and since you are reading this book we assume that you *are* smart – you will rely on these people for advice and direction for your career. Touch base with them on a regular basis. If something you consider newsworthy happens in your life – you just got married, you just had a new baby, your last movie won an Academy Award for Best Picture – tell your publicist. If you spoke to a group of students about your new book, let your publicist know. If you waded through three feet of snow to rescue a puppy, your marketing team can use that information. We could go on *ad nauseum*, but you get our drift.

If you are an indie artist, you need to gather your own team of people. We don't mean your parents or spouse or your BFFs, unless they have experience within the industry [See *pushy stage mother* above]. We mean people who understand the industry and will be honest with you about your project as well as other areas of your career, including the different parts of your press kit and promoting yourself.

They need to be believers who support you and understand your heart and the Lord's calling on your life. Your team could be as official as an honest to goodness board of directors, but it could also be an informal group of people who are committed to praying for you while at the same time offering sound advice. Regardless of how they are organized, you need to be committed to listen to them, even if you don't like what they have to say.

He, She, We

This book contains the collaborative efforts of three unique individuals, plus input from dozens of industry experts from a broad range of backgrounds. Some of the situations mentioned in these pages are things all of us have experienced. Others are unique to only one of us. To keep it simple for you, the reader [and for us, the writers], we will use third person plural pronouns [*we, us, our*] throughout most of the book. For sections that are unique to one or two of the writers, we will specify the author(s) by name.

Some of the information in this book was supplied by fellow creative people within the industry. They are all people we know personally and trust. To these, we tip our collective hat and say, "Thanks." We owe you a backscratch and, as successful networkers, we promise to repay.

Chapter One

Introductions

At some point in time, you were probably taught, or at least exposed to, the social skills involved with making proper introductions.

A proper introduction will go beyond simply sharing names. It will include enough information to help both parties feel more comfortable in each other's company.

"Betty, I'd like you to meet Wilma Flintstone; she's new to Bedrock. Wilma, this is Betty Rubble; she and her husband live next door to you. Betty, Wilma is married to Fred, who is a member of the Water Buffalo Lodge. Wilma, Betty's husband Barney is also a member of the Water Buffalo Lodge."

Beyond providing their names, you have shared

information that these two ladies have in common. They now have a starting point to get to know each other better. When it comes down to basics, promotion is about introductions. For the artist, this means letting your audience know:

- Who you are.
- What your product is.
- When your product is coming out.
- Where you are going.
- Why you are going there.
- Who you are doing this for.
- Why they should care.

Before you can tell other people who you are, however, it's important that *you* know who you are, if for no other reason than to know how you want to be introduced. As the caterpillar in "Alice in Wonderland" so succinctly inquired, "Who Are You?"

What's the point?

When Mike conducts an interview, one of his favorite opening questions to new artists is, "What's the point?"

The *point* that Mike refers to is, 'Why am I conducting this interview with you? Who are you? Why do you do what you do, and why should I care?' What he means is, 'Do you have a mission statement? Do you have a ministry, a goal, a passion? Have you had an unusual experience that people other than your mother would find interesting? Can you express it in such a way that makes me excited about it? *What's the point?'*

A few years ago, Mike and Paula interviewed an up-and-coming young band that had just charted their first hit in the Christian market. They were fresh, exuberant, talented, and eager. They had great personalities. And we had a rotten interview.

They missed the point.

"Why are you doing what you are doing?" we asked. "Why *Christian* music rather than pursuing a general market deal? What is your purpose? *What's the point?*"

They responded with looks and a shrugged, "We just want to be available to do whatever God wants us to do."

It was a nice, safe answer. It sounded like a sincere answer. We believed it was a sincere answer. But it didn't give us anything to write about. After all, as believers we all want to be available to do whatever God wants us to do. But, just exactly what did, 'Whatever God wants us to do,' mean to them?

"So," we replied, "what if your next gig is at a large church, and the youth pastor tells you they've decided they really don't need music. They are going to pay you for your time, but rather than taking the stage and making music, 'why don't you make yourselves *useful* and clean the toilets?'"

Probably not the follow-up question they were expecting.

"Well, if that's what God wanted us to do, we would do it," they stammered, and followed it up with appropriate Scripture about servanthood, and Jesus washing the disciples feet, and the first shall be last.

Another nice, safe answer; but somehow it just didn't really ring true, and, as we left the interview, we weren't sure we really believed it. After all, these guys weren't plumbers, or auto mechanics, or firefighters. They were musicians, singers, songwriters and performers. They had a job to do, and that job probably didn't involve cleaning toilets, although, "Award-Winning Christian Band Spends Weekend Cleaning Toilets," might actually have made a pretty good headline.

Body Parts

The reality is, anyone who is committed to the cause of Christ is going to want do whatever God wants them to do. That's just the nature of Christianity. But some people are called to mop floors or fix cars, and some people are called to sing, or act, or write. God calls people to different ministries.

The Apostle Paul compares it to our physical bodies. Not everyone is an eye. Not everyone is a hand. Not everyone is a foot. Not everyone is a backbone, or a pulmonary artery, or a small intestine. But every part has a specific job to do that is vitally important, and quite frankly *cannot* be done by any other part of the body. It would be pretty silly for the optic nerve to try to digest breakfast, even if it is a job that *needs* to be done. The eye is just not made for that job, no matter how 'willing' it is to be used by God.

So, we ask you again, "What's the point?" Perhaps a better question is, "What's *your* point?"

Do you love to lead praise and worship? Do you love to rock? Do you relish singing in bars, sharing the Gospel with people who would never darken the doors of a church? Or do you prefer to sing in churches to encourage believers who would never darken the doors of a bar? Are you a filmmaker who just finished your first film? Are you a speaker who likes to encourage young mothers or single fathers? Do you use comedy to open people's eyes to the wonder of God's grace? Are you a church that houses a community theater? Are you a businessman who uses your influence to encourage kids to go on short-term mission trips? Do you support an orphanage in Haiti? Did God deliver you out of a horrible situation and you want to minister to others facing a similar situation? Maybe your little brother has Down Syndrome and your passion is to raise awareness about the condition.

By answering these questions ahead of time, you will sharpen your own focus and make it easier for interviewers to help promote you and your work.

Know Your Genre

The Merriam-Webster Dictionary defines _genre_ as, "a category of artistic, musical, or literary composition characterized by a particular style, form, or content."

When Mike and Paula interview a new artist, they often will ask them what genre their music is in. It is not uncommon for artists to shrug their shoulders and reply, "We have a unique style. Our sound crosses all boundaries. We play a lot of everything. We don't want our music to be pigeon-holed into a particular genre."

That might sound sophisticated and artistic. It might even be true. But it doesn't help your potential audience, or your interviewer.

Let's say that Anna Owen walks into the local record store

to buy a copy of an album by the new group, Facing the Elephant. [For the record, Anna is a real person; we made up the name of the group, so if your band happens to be called Facing the Elephant, this is *not* about you.] Because the name of your band is not indicative of any particular genre, how will Anna know where to find it? Yes, she could ask a clerk, who should know where to find the CD - except when the store owner opened the box of Facing the Elephant CDs, he didn't know what category to put them in, so they ended up in the 'Children's Music' bin - a place the clerk never thought to look.

Yes, we also know we live in the digital information age. There aren't too many brick and mortar record stores left, but the principle is the same if Anna went to her favorite online record store. When a customer has cash-in-fist and is ready to buy, the last thing you want to do is make it hard for her.

Rather than make a movie of the week out of this scenario, just realize that beginning with the marketing team at the label and trickling down to the store owner, to the clerk, to the customer, it's important to know what genre your work fits into - even if it's metal-bluegrass-banjo-funk.

Write it Down

Questions such as "What's the point?" and "What genre do you work in?" are defining questions. The answers to these questions can help you define and refine your mission and calling. As you grapple with these questions and come up with the answers, write them down. They will become part of your mission statement or statement of purpose.

Write down everything that you can think of about what

you want to accomplish with your project, your career or your ministry. Take your time and be as detailed as you can. This is brainstorming time. Don't worry about making it sound eloquent at first; just jot down the ideas as they come to you. You can always go back later and polish them.

Read your answers out loud. Listen to how they sound. Refine your answers until you come up with a single statement that succinctly defines who you are and what you do. This is your mission statement.

Share it with your Team [If you didn't read the Prologue, go back and do it now. It explains *the Team*]. Listen to your Team's responses with an open mind; it's much better to hear someone who cares about you tell you that your statement of purpose sounds corny, hackneyed, or contrived than to end up as some writer's anecdote for a poor quote.

If your team likes it, ask why. If they don't like it, ask why. Ask if they have any suggestions for improvement. That doesn't mean you have to erase what you originally came up with. It does mean being willing to add, subtract, cut, paste and polish your mission statement until it shines like a diamond.

Be flexible. Mission statements are not written in stone. What may be true for you today might change tomorrow. Torry started out as an LA-based actor before he moved to Alaska and started writing comedy sketches. Then he moved to Tennessee and became a screenwriter. He is now commonly seen on the stage doing stand-up comedy as well as acting in films and on television while he continues honing his craft as a writer. Paula started out as a stage actress, began writing dramatic sketches for church drama teams, moved into writing reviews and feature articles, and is now an author and playwright. Mike began his career as a freelance writer, and has since branched out into acting and directing.

Who Are You?

Once you have your mission statement firmly established it is time to work on your own introduction, or biographical sketch. Your bio should be long enough to provide all the pertinent information about you but short enough to be intriguing, to make people want to ask questions about you. Keep in mind that your bio is an introduction, not a memoir.

To give you an idea of what we mean, we've included our own introductions:

Meet Paula K. Parker
Instead of the typical writer's resume, Paula created a document entitled *About the Author: Paula K. Parker,* which she includes with her press kit as a resource for potential interviewers. It begins with a short introduction and follows with a list of the major writing she has done. Here is her introduction.

Paula K. Parker has been writing as long as she can remember. With a poet father, writer mother, and a story-teller grandmother, she has always been comfortable in the world of words. Early training in music and theater led Paula to a life-long love for the arts. This passion eventually brought her to Nashville, TN, where she - along with her writer husband, Mike - helped establish Carpenter's Playhouse and Lamplighter's Theatre Company.

A stint teaching in the public school system, along with seventeen years of homeschooling her five children, has resulted in not only a quick wit and a unique sense of humor, but also the ability to effectively communicate ideas on a wide range of subjects to a broad range of age groups.

Since 1995, Paula has been a professional freelance writer with more than 1,000 articles, sketches, plays, scripts and books to her credit. She has written for such highly-regarded national publications as "Christian Single," "Christian Health," "Family Fun" (Disney), "Living with Teenagers," the "National Drama Service," "ParentLife," "Clarity," "Release Ink," "Profile," "Bible Express," and "HomeLife" magazines. She contributed to Thomas Nelson's New York Times Best-Selling Bible-zine, *Becoming.* Her stage plays include adaptations of the Jane Austen classics, "Pride & Prejudice" and "Sense & Sensibility" as well as numerous original works.

Online she has written for Crosswalk.com and LifeWay.com, and currently serves as the National Christian Entertainment Examiner for Examiner.com and Editor for the online entertainment magazine, BuddyHollywood.com. In 2010, her first novel was released, "YHWH: The Flood, The Fish and The Giant," co-written with NY Times best-selling author, GP Taylor.

Meet Mike Parker
Mike Parker is an award-winning freelance writer, actor, director, novelist, playwright & screenwriter. A BA degree in Bible and Philosophy, a stint as an officer with the US Army Special Forces (Green Berets), a career as a stock broker during the great bull market of the eighties, and an entrepreneurial plunge into the uncertain world of television syndication have all combined to give him a

unique outlook on the world. Blessed [or cursed] with an insatiable curiosity he is voracious reader, questioner, ponderer.

The year 1993 brought Mike from Texas to Nashville, TN where he, along with his playwright wife, Paula, helped establish Carpenter's Playhouse, a local community theatre. Together they now serve on the board of Lamplighter's Theatre in Smyrna, TN. With the creative juices flowing from the theatre and the proximity of both the music and publishing industries, Mike turned his attention to his old flame, writing. His efforts paid off as more than 2,000 of his articles, celebrity profiles, CD, book & theater reviews, and poetry have been published by such national periodicals as "Campus Life," "Today's Christian Parent," "Vibrant Life," and "CCM." His articles have been featured on the covers of such national publications as "HomeLife," "Christian Single," "Stand Firm," "Bible Express," "Living With Teenagers," "7Ball," and "Release" Magazines.

Meet Torry Martin

Torry Martin is a writer, actor, comedian, speaker, author, storyteller and teacher who has delighted audiences and readers for years with his zany personality and warm heart. This hilarious transplanted Alaskan and self-confessed Hippie for the Holy One uses his creative way of looking at life to draw people in and quench their thirst for laughter, while at the same time imparting important spiritual truths.

He is a member of the Christian Comedy Association and a two-time Christian Artists Gospel Music Association Grand Prize Winner for his acting and writing abilities. More recently, he was awarded the Grand Prize for creating the best "Life Lessons" commercial for The Learning Channel.

Torry writes for the "Adventures in Odyssey" radio series for Focus on the Family and is the creator of Wooton Bassett, a popular character in the series. He additionally writes a regularly featured humor column for Christian periodicals "On Course" and "Club House." He travels across the country speaking and performing standup comedy at a variety of Christian events.

Torry regularly teaches at Christian writers and filmmakers conferences on topics that include "Sketch Writing 101," "Comedy in Action/Show me The Funny," "Discovering Your Calling and Finding Your Gift," "The Art of Collaborative Writing," and of course, "Shameless Self Promotion and Networking."

The Mini-Intro

In addition to a full-blown introduction, which you will include as an integral part of your press kit, it is helpful to write and polish your own two-sentence introduction. This should be one of the first things you put in your press kit. Your mini-intro will be used by the interviewer or emcee to read before you go air or before you come out on stage. A two-sentence intro is intentionally short so it can be written on an index card that is small enough for the emcee to hold in the palm of her hand.

"It is better for your audience to be impressed with your performance than with your introduction," Torry says. "The worst introduction I ever got came from a friend who told the audience, 'Torry Martin is the funniest comedian you will ever hear!' There is no way I could ever live up to that kind of hype. I could see members of the audience crossing their arms as if to say, 'Okay, big boy, prove it!'

"The second worst introduction I ever got came from a person who had never met me and had never seen me perform. He said, 'I've been told Torry Martin is really funny, but I've never seen him, so I don't know. Here he is.' Since you never know who is going to introduce you, it is imperative that you have a two-sentence introduction that is easy for anyone to read. Your job, at that point, is to live up to your own press."

Torry's standard introduction is – "Torry Martin is an award winning actor, comedian, and writer who created the character of Wooten Basset for "Adventures in Odyssey." Please welcome the Hippie for the Holy One."

Chapter Two

The Press Kit

If you're new to the industry, you may not have any idea what a press kit is. Even if you know what a press kit is, you might not know what a *good* press kit should contain.

Here's the skinny:
A press kit is a collection of promotional materials that is provided to media outlets, performance venues, promoters and other influencers, usually as part of a publicity campaign. A press kit serves as an introduction to the artist, project or event.

Physical press kits can be expensive to produce and expensive to send, so use them judiciously. Electronic press kits may also be expensive to produce, but they cost little to distribute online. It is a good idea to have both.

There are two scenarios when you might send out a press kit:

Scenario One: A Media Outlet Asks For It

Mike has been contacted by BuddyHollywood.com to write an article about this amazing Christian comedian, Torry Martin. Mike contacts Torry's publicist or - if Torry doesn't have a publicist - he contacts Torry directly. Mike explains that he has been assigned to write an article about Torry and needs to set up an interview. Torry – or Torry's publicist – not only schedules the interview, but sends Mike one of Torry's press kits. The press kit is chock-full of fascinating information that will help Mike prepare for the interview, and later will serve as a basis for his article.

Scenario Two: Your Promotional Pitch

Paula opens her daily mail to find a press kit about this amazing Christian comedian, Torry Martin. The press kit includes a cover letter that mentions Torry is available for interview. Paula has heard of Torry, but knows little about him. She receives a dozen or more press kits in the mail each week, not counting the multitude that clutter her email inbox. Most hard copy press kits end up in a large pile in the corner of her office, awaiting the time when she has no other pressing matters to attend to. However, something about Torry's press kit catches her eye, and rather than tossing it into the slush pile with the others, she takes the time to sit down and look through it. Intrigued by this handsome and talented young man, she decides to write an article about Torry for BuddyHollywood.com.

The primary difference in these two scenarios is; one press kit is requested while the other is sent cold with high hopes and fingers crossed. As mentioned before, physical press kits are expensive to produce and mail. While they are an invaluable resource in either situation, if cost is a factor, save your hard copy press kits for people who request them, and do your cold calling with your electronic press kit, known in the industry as your EPK.

Regardless of whether you send a physical or electronic press kit, it is absolutely essential that the content inside the press kit be fresh, up to date and professional in appearance. Every artist's situation is unique, so every press kit should be tailored to that situation. A press kit for a film might contain production notes, while a press kit for a book might include favorable reviews of your previous novels.

If you are involved in multiple art forms or have multiple projects, you probably need more than one press kit. Regardless of what kind of project you are promoting or how many different art forms you are involved with, there are some basics that every press kit needs.

Press Kit Check List

Pictures

The old saying, _"A picture is worth a thousand words,"_ is absolutely true for a press kit. We were not exaggerating when we said that Paula and Mike receive a dozen or more press kits each week. [We were exaggerating, however, when we said that they are stacked in piles in Paula's office; they are actually stacked in piles in Mike's office. But we digress...] Your picture should be the first thing a journalist sees when she opens your press kit.

Good quality pictures catch the eye and give your press kit

a fighting chance to not end up gathering dust in the corner of Mike's – or some other journalist's – office. There are two types of pictures that appear in a press kit; the headshot and the picture page.

Headshot

A professional quality 8x10 is an essential part of a press kit for anyone in the creative arts whether you are an individual artist or a group. If you can afford it, have your headshot taken by a professional photographer. This can be pricey. You might find a photographer who can deliver the goods for an $85 sitting fee, but a good headshot from a pro, including hair and makeup [yes, this applies to guys as well as girls] can set you back several hundred dollars, particularly if you rely on the photographer to provide you with reproductions.

Keep in mind that photographs by professional photographers are usually copyrighted material. You need to understand what kind of reproduction rights you are buying before you sit for your headshot. You will typically only be able to get reproduction and press rights to one photo unless you buy more. Always respect the copyright. It is how your photographer makes a living.

You may need to pay for the services of a stylist or makeup artist, but we're not talking 'glamour shots' here. You are looking for a good representation of *you*. You can hire a professional makeup artist to be on set for your photo shoot, but it will cost you. You can save a few bucks by scheduling an appointment at the fine makeup counter at your local department store.

If you can't afford to pay the photographer's going rate, get creative. *You are creative, aren't you?* Talk to him. Is there something you can offer in exchange? Barter is a time honored tradition. Maybe you can work out a trade. That's how Mike and Paula got their first headshots.

"We met a professional photographer when our daughter Rachael was modeling," Mike recalls. "We chatted with the photographer while Rachael was changing for the shoot. The photographer asked what we did for a living. When he discovered Paula and I were writers, he offered to do a photo shoot in exchange for a professional bio."

That photographer turned out to be Allen Clark, who a dozen years later, took the authors' photos for the back copy of this book.

Consider contacting your local newspaper to see if they have a news photographer who hires out freelance. Ask to see some of his work. If it's good, you might be able to hire him for significantly less than a studio photographer, although you may not get all the bells and whistles. In addition to the photographer's professional fee, you will be responsible for the cost of purchasing, developing, and printing the film. Even if he shoots digital, you will still have to pay for your prints. On the positive side, since it is a work for hire gig, you will own the negatives and the copyright to the pictures, so you can use any shot you want without the legal hassles.

A third option is to check with your local college's photography classes. Photography students have a certain number of assignments they have to complete, so they may agree to do your headshot for a nominal fee or even for free. Having their work in a professional press kit helps them build their resume, so it's is a plus for them as well. Just make sure to give them photo credit.

The advent of digital photography has placed extraordinary photo technology into the hands of the common people. Avid amateurs who are trying to turn their hobby into a business may be willing to do a photo shoot for a reduced price in order to build their portfolio. As with college students, you will be responsible for covering the cost of printing the photos.

Regardless of where you find your photographer, it is absolutely imperative to make sure your photographer can deliver the goods. It is also imperative that you are comfortable with your photographer. If you are not comfortable with your photographer, walk away. If you don't seem to be able to communicate effectively with your photographer, walk away. If you just have a gut feeling that this photographer is not the right fit, trust your feeling and walk away.

"I came from the other side of the industry before I became a professional photographer," Allen Clark says. "I was an artist development agent for the William Morris Agency, which is one of the largest talent agencies in the world. I was the one who received all those press kits. Nine times out of 10 when it looked like the photo was done by the artist's cousin, the music was dreadful. It seemed like those two things went hand in hand. If a person had a good idea of what a good presentation for their photo was, nine times of out 10, their music sounded good. The bottom line is, when someone appears to know what they are doing, they probably do, and it translates across genres."

You may not know what a good headshot is supposed to look like. A quick way to see what the entertainment industry thinks is a good headshot is to go online and check out talent agency websites. Find headshots that you like.

Make a note of them. Show them to your photographer.

"If your photographer can see what you are looking for, she has a better chance of getting inside your head, and she'll be more likely to deliver a great end product," Allen says.

Once you get your proofs back, it is likely that you will have a lot of photos that look remarkably similar. It can be a daunting task to pick the best shot out of a bunch of good shots. Allen recommends showing the pictures to your peers or colleagues who may not see you on a day to day basis. This is where your team comes in.

"Get a pair of fresh eyes on your pictures," Allen says. "You probably want to stay away from family members who have seen you day in and day out. They are too close to the subject. You want someone who doesn't remember when you had a nose ring or when you were a redhead."

Remember that turnabout is fair play. If you get a great headshot at a discounted price, grab a handful of the photographer's business cards. When someone tells you, "Hey, great headshot!" don't just say, "Thank you." Hand them one of your photographer's business cards. Tell your colleagues how great your photographer was to work with. Sing the photographer's praise, but don't say, "You should call Polly Roid; she did my headshots for free!" Polly may have done a cut-rate photo shoot for you, but that doesn't mean she'll do it for someone else.

"Technology has reduced the cost of photographic equipment to the point that anyone with a cell phone thinks they are a photographer," Allen quips. "While everyone has to start somewhere, you probably don't want that guy shooting your headshot. The good news is; competition has driven prices down, so you won't have to spend as much as you used to for a good headshot. The bad news is, there are a lot of amateurs out there who think they are professionals, and it is easy to pay way too much for a bad headshot."

Preparing for the Photo Shoot

As with most things in life, when it comes to your photo shoot *proper prior preparation prevents pitifully poor performance.* Preparing for the photo shoot is almost as important has having a great photographer. Notice that we said, 'almost.' We've seen some great photographers work miracles with less than optimum subjects. Still, whatever you can do to help the photographer increases your chances for a great head shot.

When it comes to your clothes, simple is better. You know that super cool shirt with a psychedelic print? Don't wear it for the photo shoot. Ladies, be aware of your neckline. You want the eyes drawn to your face, not to your cleavage.

"It is always better to wear solids," Allen says. "Your face is the thing that needs to be pointed to. Your headshot is about your face and your personality, not your clothing. You want your audience to notice you, not your clothes. No whites, no reds, no bold prints. Black works for most people, but you may need to try it out because some people just can't wear it. Bottom line - if it doesn't work, don't wear it."

Don't wear your photo shoot clothes to the photo shoot. Carry them with you in a garment bag and change when you arrive at the venue. You don't want a wrinkle from the car's seatbelt shoulder strap showing up in your headshot.

Don't limit yourself to a single look. Take several changes of clothing and rely on your photographer for suggestions on what looks best on camera.

"A good photographer will be able to tell you when something doesn't look right on camera," Allen notes. "Just one more reason to go with seasoned pro if you can."

A word about wearing logos: don't. Logos can date your photo. Logos may prevent you from getting cast by a competing company. As a matter of fact, just stay away from writing of any kind on your clothing. Your best bet is to stick with solid colors - except for the aforementioned solid white and solid red.

Keep any jewelry unobtrusive, for the same reason you refrain from wearing busy prints - you want the attention on your face.

Although it is not absolutely required, you may consider engaging the services of a makeup artist. This goes for the guys as well as the gals. A good makeup artist can do something about those capillaries on your nose, those dark circles under your eyes, and that red splotch that came up in the middle of the night.

Ladies, your headshot is not the appropriate place to display for your stunning evening/party makeup. We've said it before, and we'll say it again, this is not a glamour shot. If you choose to do your own makeup, apply it with a light hand using neutral colors. The goal is to have someone think, *"What a great face!"* not *"What great makeup!"*

"With the advent of photo editing software, makeup is not as essential as it used to be, but that doesn't mean you don't need it," Allen says. "When I'm on a photo shoot and there is a makeup artist available, it makes my life as a photographer, a whole lot easier."

Think like a Boy Scout and *Be Prepared* by carrying an emergency kit with you to every photo shoot. Your emergency kit should include the things you need to touch up your hair and makeup - a comb/brush, bobby pins, safety pins [they have a million uses, trust us on this one] hairspray, and makeup. Get some oil blotting tissues; you can find them in the makeup supply section at most drug stores. They can help remove the shine from your face, preventing the need to add more powder. For those of you like Mike, who have, shall we say, less than a full head of hair, you might want to carry some translucent powder, to cut down on the reflection from your pate.

Headshots Odds and Ends

Even if your photographer has a professional studio with backdrops, it never hurts to take some of the pictures outside. These pictures can look less staged and more natural. Plus, you don't want to have only one picture that you send out each time. Using a variety of pictures can keep your press kit fresh.

Paula notes the effect of getting regular press releases about an artist with the same ol' headshot attached.

"When I get multiple press releases about the same artist, and the artist's press photo is the same, I have a tendency think the information in the press release is just more of the same. I may hit 'delete' without even reading the press release, because it appears to be old news."

The standard for television and film headshot is color while actors in the theatrical world still use black & white headshots. If you only have the budget for one or the other, choose color. You can always digitally convert a color headshot to a B&W headshot. It doesn't hurt to include both color and B&W photos in your press kit, as some media outlets, such as local newspapers, tend to print most photos in black & white.

Remember, your photographer is a part of your network and you want to maintain a professional relationship with her. Ask your photographer questions to get to know her. This will make you more comfortable with her, and it will make her more comfortable with you. A comfortable photographer takes better pictures. Always send your photographer a thank you card.

Important Note: Once you have your head shot, remember this picture represents you to casting agents or event sponsors. While this is not a written in stone photo, if the cover of your CD or the back of your novel shows you with long hair and a beard, people are going to expect to see you with long hair and a beard.

On the next page we've included an example of an excellent headshot from our friend, actress and author, Nancy Stafford. Nancy's original headshot is in color, and can be viewed at her website, www.NancyStafford.com. Note the simplicity of her sweater, the absence of jewelry and the uncomplicated background. There is nothing in this headshot that distracts your eyes from her lovely face.

Nancy Stafford

Picture Page

A picture page is a collection of no more than four snapshots on a single sheet of paper. One or two of these pictures should be of you performing. If you are not a performing artist, look for something that reflects your art. An author can have a picture taken of him seated in front of his computer or at a book signing. A filmmaker can have a picture of him speaking with a cameraman. A songwriter can have a picture of her sitting at a piano. A speaker can have a picture taken with some people from a recent event. The picture page represents you as an artist. Pictures on this page can show a lot more attitude and passion than your headshot.

"A professional headshot is usually not thematic," Allen notes. "It's just *'me looking my best.'* Promotional shots are going to be more thematic. Whether these shots are about theme or about attitude, the important thing to remember is, don't take yourself too seriously. Don't look too deep into it."

The picture page should include a picture of you and your family. If you're not married, then a picture of you and your parents, you and your sister/brother, or you and your dog; something that you would include in a Christmas card. This picture represents you as a regular person.

The fourth picture should be of you with a well-known artist, DJ, media personality or an individual who is easily recognizable in your field. This is not a fan picture and it is not narcissistic. This picture is designed to establish your credibility in the eyes of your industry. If you see Steven Curtis Chapman in the mall and he graciously allows you to take a picture with him, do *not* include this on your picture page [and we are not advocating approaching celebrities in the mall; they have a life, for cryin' out loud - let them live it]. We are talking about a picture that is taken of you with a news reporter who interviewed you, in front of the station logo if possible, or a shot of you backstage with Michael W. Smith after a benefit concert.

Like a headshot, the pictures on a picture page need to be changed out frequently enough to keep them fresh. If your infant son in the family picture is now entering first grade, it is time to change that picture.

If you have a hard time picking out appropriate pictures for your press kit, leave the decision to your board or team.

Bio

Just like a professional quality headshot, a well-written bio is *a must* for a press kit. You bio should be no more than two pages long, and should provide a potential interviewer will all the information she needs to generate some interesting questions about you and your current project.

A good bio should contain:

- Your introduction [from Chapter One]
- Your artistic history.
- An in-depth look at your latest project, including overarching themes, inspirations, and tidbits of information not included in the actual project. You should provide enough information so the reader knows what to expect, but not enough to giveaway the punch line or ending.
- Your mission statement. This should be a brief one or two sentence statement about what you want to

accomplish with your ministry. Your mission statement should be incorporated into the bio. It is usually not something that you have labeled at the beginning or ending of the bio.

- Accolades. Some might consider it bragging to list the awards you have won. But awards, particularly those given by your peers within your industry, increase your credibility.
- Your website.
- Your contact information. If you are represented by a talent agent, a booking agent or manager use their contact information; otherwise use your own unique industry contact info.

"It's a good idea to have a separate telephone number, email address, and mailing address such as a post office box to use for business purposes," Torry notes. "Keeping your professional contact information separate from your personal contact information help protect your personal privacy."

Side note: Make sure your voicemail message sounds pleasant and professional. Even if your performance persona is wild and crazy, when it comes to business, people usually prefer to deal with sane and normal.

Your incoming voicemail message should sound something like this:

"You've reached the office of <u>insert your name or band's name here.</u> I am unable to take your call now. Please leave your name, number, and a brief message, and I'll get back with you as soon as possible. Thank you and have a wonderful day."

Depending upon your art form, you might need more than one bio. Mike and Torry are both writers and actors, and they have separate bios to reflect those skills.

Bio writing is an art form unto itself. If you can afford it, you are better off hiring an industry pro. While it is unlikely that you will find a listing for 'Professional Bio Writers' in your local yellow pages, believe us, they are out there. Check with your local ad agencies or public relations firms. Chances are they have a stable of freelancers they use on a regular basis. Or just ask other artists that you have a relationship with who they used.

You can also go online to websites of creative folks who are similar in style and substance to you. Read their bio. In some cases they will include the writer's name. If not, it doesn't hurt to drop the artist an email. Honestly compliment their bio and ask them if they would be willing to share the name of the writer.

Rates for a professional bio are all over the map. 2011 rates in the Nashville, TN area range from $350 to $600, but rates in New York or LA may be dramatically higher. Rates may also vary significantly based on the bio writer's level of experience or your relationship with the bio writer.

Bio writing is a tricky skill. If you have never had a bio written before, you may not know what you are looking for until you see it. This can drive bio writers nuts. Trust us on this one. We've written tons of bios, and there is nothing more frustrating to a bio writer than a client who doesn't know what they want. It's like throwing darts in the dark and hoping you at least hit the board.

Before you contact a writer, you need to have a firm idea

about who you are as an artist, and what you want your bio to be about. Make a list of things you want included in your bio and give it to the writer. Be sure to keep a copy of the list for yourself to refer back to when you read over the first draft.

Make sure both you and the writer understand what services are being offered, what services are expected, what kind of fee is being charged and when payment is expected before you engage the writer's services. You don't want any surprises when you get the invoice.

A professional bio writer's package will typically include the interview, the first draft and one or two rounds of edits. Some writers may offer the interview, the first draft, one full rewrite and one additional tweak. They may charge more for additional changes. If you don't know what you are looking for going in, this could get real expensive, real fast. It's like going into the studio to rehearse. You can do it, but the meter is running and you will pay the piper.

Before you engage a bio writer's services, be absolutely sure you understand the payment terms. Some writers will ask for half up front, particularly if they have never done business with you before. This is not unreasonable, and you should not be offended.

On the flip side, if you have never worked with this person before, you should check them out before you fork over any of your hard earned cash. Check their references. Check out samples of their work. Read bios they have written to make sure their work fits your style. Above all, make sure you are comfortable with the writer. If you are not, walk away.

Let the writer know how soon you need the finished bio,

but if you need it quick, be prepared to make yourself available to the writer...and be prepared to pay a premium. Any bio writer worth his salt already has plenty of other work lined up. You have to pay if you want to go to the front of the line.

A bio interview should take at least an hour, either in person or by phone, but it could last for several hours, depending on how in-depth the writer needs to go.

The writer will likely record the interview and transcribe it once he gets home, although we know writers who can type while they talk. Transcribing is a tedious and time consuming task than can take three to four times the amount of time required for the interview. Once the transcription is complete, it can take several more hours for the writer to finish the first draft.

A good bio write can turn a finished bio around in a week or less, but only if you are available to review the draft for any necessary changes. Don't be afraid to ask for changes, but make sure you have a clear vision of what you want. It is helpful to the writer if you ask for all the changes at one time, rather than piecemeal.

If you can't afford a professional bio writer, check with your local college to see if it has a public relations course in their mass communications department. The professor should be able to recommend students she feels could write a solid bio.

As with the photographer, send your bio writer a thank you note. This not only builds a relationship - which makes it easier to work with them in the future - it has other potential benefits for you. Many bio writers, such as Mike and Paula, also write freelance in the entertainment field. Like most people, they enjoy writing feature articles about people with whom they have a positive relationship. A paid bio may lead to unpaid publicity in the form of feature articles or reviews.

Writing Your Own Bio... [insert scary music here]

Some creative people feel they can write their own bio - and they may very well be able to - but it is not a given. While you may be a great writer and have no problem writing a bio for another person, it is a different animal when you are looking in the mirror.

"Several years ago I interviewed a popular Christian singer/songwriter," Paula says. "In preparing for the interview, I read her bio. It was *awful*; the writing style was amateurish and the bio included unnecessary and irrelevant information that no one except her family would be interested in. During our interview, the artist casually mentioned that she had written her own bio. 'I can write songs,' she shrugged, 'so I figured I could write a bio.'" *Wrong!*

Mike has written bios for such popular artists as Big Daddy Weave, Carmen, Margaret Becker, Aaron Shust, The Waiting, Big Tent Revival, Nicole C. Mullen, Sandy Patti, Wayne Watson and a multitude of others, but struggles to write his own bio.

"Even if you are a good writer, there are numerous challenges to writing your own bio," Mike declares. "One of the most significant challenges is, you don't see yourself as others see you. It's like listening to yourself on a digital recorder. It doesn't sound like the voice you hear in your head. If you think self promotion is hard, try saying all those great things you read in bios of other people about yourself. Now try doing it with a straight face. It's tough, I tell ya!"

If you have no other recourse than to write your own bio, our best advice is to take your time. Work it over and polish it until it shines like silver. Your bio is too important to slap it together in an hour. Show it to your Team. Listen to their advice and tweak it as necessary.

To give you an idea of what a good bio should look like, we've included one from our friend, actress Jenn Gotzon.

JENN GOTZON

Actress **JENN GOTZON** is a small-town girl who has big dreams of making a difference in people's lives. Raised in the suburbs of Allentown, PA, **GOTZON** has persistently pursued her passion for film acting to play complex characters who find hope in the climax of the storyline. She began performing right out of high school; appearing in a murder mystery dinner theater, entertaining at Walt Disney World and competing in the Miss America pageant system.

After studying at The New York Conservatory for Dramatic Arts, **GOTZON** moved to Los Angeles and landed a string of bit parts in big productions like Ang Lee's **HULK,** Sundance pleaser **500 DAYS OF SUMMER,** Sean William Scott starrer **ROLE MODELS** along with Emmy-winning TV series **PUSHING DAISIES** and **HOUSE.** Big parts in smaller productions came her way, too, including 168 Film Festival 2008 best film winner **STAINED** that earned her the fest's best actress award for her lead role as a political prisoner in a futuristic society. At the 2008 Wildwood By-The-Sea (NJ) Film Festival she was named Rising Star of the year for her leading lady turn in the speed-dating romantic comedy short **CHEMISTRY** whose fest director Paul Russo described **GOTZON** as "having the acting depth of Kate Winslet and the charisma of Reese Witherspoon."

The Pennsylvania native got her big break, ironically, on Pennsylvania Avenue in Ron Howard's 2009 best picture Oscar nominee **FROST/NIXON**, playing the president's daughter Tricia Nixon. Since then, GOTZON's dream has started to come true, beginning with her portraying heroine Beatrice alongside Eric Roberts as her love Dante in docudrama **DANTE'S INFERNO DOCUMENTED** based on the legendary The Divine Comedy. Last year, she starred in five feature films (in chron order): romantic mystery-drama **DOONBY** opposite "The Dukes of Hazzard" star John Schneider; political-thriller **DRAGON DAY** about a Chinese cyber-takeover of the U.S.; French and Indian War drama **ALONE YET NOT ALONE**, in which she plays an historical British captive; faith-based musical **SEPTEMBER SKIES**; and family-friendly comedic-drama **GOD'S COUNTRY,** directed by her husband Chris Armstrong and set to be distributed by Sony.

More recently, **GOTZON** commenced principal photography on the spoken word poetry slam drama **THE DIARY OF BABINEAUX** in Austin, TX. Currently, she and her writer-director-Super-Bowl-commercial-finalist hubby are working on a New Orleans action-thriller about the significance of life produced by their production company Elysian Pictures and Brown Pelican Films. All are socially relevant films that endeavor to make a difference in people's lives.

GOTZON's ultimate passion is impacting and inspiring audiences through the message behind the roles she plays. With this goal, she developed a motivational mentor-outreach program, "Inspiring Audiences," through which she speaks to students, screens her movies and shares her testimony on overcoming life's obstacles with prayer and perseverance in hopes to encourage them to find their passion in life and live their dreams.

Professional Resume

When you apply for a job in almost any industry, chances are the interviewer will ask to see your resume. There are many different types of formats for resumes depending on the industry that you work in. The entertainment industry is no different. You need to have a properly formatted resume, and you may need more than one if you work in multiple creative media. Our friend, actress Nancy Stafford allowed us to use her professional resume as an example.

Nancy Stafford
SAG/AFTRA
www.nancystafford.com   310-613-6393   email: ns@nancystafford.com

TELEVISION (partial list)

The Mentalist	Guest Star	CBS
Judging Amy	Guest Star	CBS
ER	Guest Star	NBC
Frasier	Guest Star	NBC
Matlock	Series Regular (5 years)	NBC
Sidekicks	Series Regular (1 year)	ABC
St. Elsewhere	Series Regular (3 years)	NBC
The Doctors	Series Regular (2 years)	NBC

FILM

Christmas with a Capital C	Supporting	Vision Scape Studios
The Wager	Supporting	Eagle Rock Productions
The Proverb	Supporting	Todd Albertson Prod
Destiny	Supporting	Postmodern Parables

MOVIES FOR TELEVISION

Deadly Invasion	Starring	FOX
Moment of Truth: Child Too Many	Starring	NBC
The Last Electric Knight	Starring	ABC

HOSTING
Love, Marriage, & Stinkin' Thinkin' Weekly Talk Show
        Syndicated (1 season)
Main Floor   Fashion/Lifestyle Magazine
        Syndicated (10 seasons)
Great Day America   Live Daily Talk Show   PAX-TV
CREATION Health   DVD Seminar Series   Florida Hospital
Travel Show   Ministry of Tourism, IsraelSyndicated

VOICE-OVER (partial list)
Mattel--video game, PBS--documentary narration, The Learning Company--
educational videos, SAT-7 --non-profit donor DVD campaign, Main Floor --
TV series. Commercial list upon request

THEATRE
Present Laughter	Joanna	Melrose Theatre LA,CA
Almost Perfect	Boots	Burt Reynolds Theatre, FL
Thanksgiving	Vanessa	Powerhouse Theatre, LA,CA

TRAINING
Joanne Baron/D W Brown, Milton Katselas, Gordon Hunt, Stella Adler-NYC

Principle in over 250 commercials
Media Trainer/Corporate Consultant
Published Author of two books
Previous career in Public Relations
Motivational/Conference Speaker
Bachelor's Degree Journalism, Univ. of Florida

Height: 5'9"   Hair: Blonde   Eyes: Blue

Representation—Los Angeles:
Hosting & Broadcasting/Commercial/V-O: AKA Talent (323) 965-5600
Theatrical: Defining Artists (818) 753-2405

Representation--Florida and Southeast:
Theatrical/Commercial/Hosting/Print
Runways The Talent Group— (305) 538-3529 / (504) 214-2408

Endorsements/Reference Letters

In the old days you had to have references to get a job - any job. In our contemporary transitory society, references have taken a backseat to credentials in many occupations, but they are still a valuable resource in the entertainment industry.

Look on the back cover or inside flap of almost any book and chances are you see one or more celebrity endorsements. Look on the any movie poster and you'll see a quote in big, block letters - **STUPENDOUS! AMAZING! BEST FILM IN YEARS!** - followed by some reviewer's name in teeny tiny print.

When it comes to the creative world, people want to know that other people in positions of authority have validated your work. If you are a performing artist, whenever you perform, ask the concert promoter to write a letter of reference. Get one every time you perform. Include a few of the best reference letters in your press kit. Lift some quotes from these reference letters and create an endorsement page to include with your press kit.

Fact Sheet

For performing artists, or writers on a book tour, a fact sheet is a *one-page* list – think *bullet points* - that opens with your abbreviated introduction, provides all the pertinent details about your upcoming appearances or performances, and ends with a summary of what you have accomplished or where you have performed.

A fact sheet is a necessity, especially if you will be doing a lot of work promoting yourself to radio stations. DJs seldom have the time to look through a full press kit and then weed out the most relevant facts for their listeners. They live in a world of sound bites. Make a DJ's job easy and you will make a friend.

We've included a copy of Torry's fact sheet on the next page to give you an idea what we are talking about. Notice how each paragraph is a separate sound bite that can stand on its own. Each acts as an independent unit that your interviewer can use as a launching point.

Torry Martin
P.O. Box 397
Sparta,TN 38583
Contact for Booking: (865) 774-4444
tennesseetorry@yahoo.com
www.torrymartin.com

Torry Martin is a screenwriter, humor columnist, actor, comedian, speaker, author, storyteller and teacher.

Torry's most recent book is called "Shameless Self- Promotion" and was co-written with Paula K. Parker and Mike Parker. It is a book designed to help Christian creatives become their own public relations expert.

He is a two-time Christian Artists Gospel Music Association Grand Prize Winner for his acting and writing abilities. He is also a three-time award winner for the 48 Hour Film Project in Nashville being voted Best Actor twice and Best Writer once.

Torry has written numerous episodes of the award-winning Adventures in Odyssey audio series produced by Focus on the Family. He is also the creator of Wooton Bassett, a popular character in the series.

He writes humor columns for a variety of national Christian periodicals *Clubhouse, On Course,* and *Enrichment Journal.*

Martin has had the great pleasure of co-writing several screenplays with his good friend Marshal Younger. He is collaborating on several new fiction novels with several talented authors including Rene Gutteridge, Paula K. Parker, PeggySue Welles, Doug Peterson, Larry Leech and Nicole Rivera.

Torry travels nationally as a speaker and teacher at a variety of Christian film maker and writer conferences, He also travels extensively performing his "Torry Stories" stand-up comedy at a variety of Christian events.

Torry is the author of 7 comedy sketch books published by Lillenas Drama Publishers.

Torry earned the nick name "Moose" when collecting moose droppings and making jewelry out of it to sell to tourists in Alaska. He was working as a camp host for Alaska State Parks and living in a remote cabin on The Last Frontier when he rededicated his life to Christ.

To learn more about Torry, please visit his website at www.torrymartin.com

Press Clips

Press clips are copies of articles written about you. Cut the original out of the magazine or newspaper. If the top of the page does not list the name of the periodical and the date, carefully cut and tape it on the article. Scan the articles and upload them to the 'News' page on your website. If the article appeared online you can do a simple 'screen print.'

Store the articles on your hard drive. When you put together a press kit, print up three to five of your most recent press clips. Most people won't make through more than a few of your clips, and including more will only make your press kit bulky and more expensive to mail.

Always respect the copyright of the original publication. If you need to make copies, be sure to obtain a release form from the original publication granting you permission to reproduce the article for your press kit. Make a copy of the permission slip and keep it with the original copy of the press clip. You will need it when you make copies to comply with copyright laws.

Quote Page

A quote page is a vital tool that lets people know what others are saying about your ministry and performance. You can lift quotes off of your Judge's critiques, reviews, reference letter, newspaper or magazine articles about you, or from personal correspondence from fans. Add to your quote page as new quotes come in. Once you get enough quotes to fill a page start replacing some of the older quotes with newer quotes to keep it fresh and current. Pull two to four recent quotes from your quote page to include on any flyers that you send out.

Oh, by the way - you can forget all that junk about, *I don't care what you say about me as long as you spell my name right.* Yes, you do want them to spell your name right, but you really *do* care what they say about you. At least you really *should* care. Do we really need to say that you only want to include positive quotes?

Song by Song

Recording artists may wish to include a list of the songs from their most recent project, with a bit of history behind each song - why it was written; what it means to the artist. The song-by-song may include all or part of the lyrics.

Suggested Interview Questions

Although suggested interview questions are totally appropriate for any creative person's press kit, they are especially important for authors. While an interviewer can listen to a CD in less than an hour, while they are driving to work, it takes a serious commitment for the interviewer to work her way through a 400-page novel. Most interviewers simply will not take the time. No slam on interviewers here. We all have busy lives and have to make choices about how we invest our time. But you still want your interviewer to sound intelligent. Providing her with suggested questions results in two big benefits - you've just made her life easier [one less thing she has to think about], and you've just made your life easier [you already know the answers to the suggested questions].

Business Cards

Business cards are an inexpensive necessity of the business. Not only should you carry them with you everywhere you go, you should include one in your press kit. Paper clip one to the pocket of the folder, to your headshot or to your bio.

Some folders have slots on the inside pocket for business cards. As with bios, you might need more than one business card. Mike and Paula have several, including one for WordCrafts, their independent publishing house, another for BuddyHollywood.com, their online entertainment magazine, and yet another for their work as freelance writers.

Everyone has business card. They provide all the contact information people need to get in touch when they need your services. They are easy to give out, easy to take, easy to get lost in the stack of other business cards and easy to throw away. You want people to keep your business card, so you need a way to make your card stand out. Let's face it; most of us remember faces better than we remember names. One easy and inexpensive way to separate your card from the plethora of other business cards is to include your photo on your business card.

On the next page we've include Torry's business card as an example. Keep in mind that the original is in color.

Torry's business card uses an extroverted font for his name, which gives you an instant clue about both his role as a comedian. The front of his card provides his pertinent contact information - telephone, mailing address, website, email - in a simple, easy to read font. The back of his card succinctly states his business - Actor, Author, Comedian, Writer.

Torry's photo is a professional headshot. It captures his personality and conveys a sense of warmth and friendship.

Some actors we know use one entire side of their business card for their headshot, and use the back of the card for their contact information.

Regardless of what format you choose, make sure your information is present in a way that people don't have to work to figure it out. Simple fonts and clean lines work best.

Reviewer Product

Since the press kit is promoting your art, it should include a copy of it. If you are an author, the press kit should include a reviewer's copy of your book. If you are a singer, it should have a copy of your CD. If you're a speaker, comic or actor, the press kit should include a videotape of a performance.

Including hard copies of your product in your press kit can be expensive. Fortunately we live in the age of digital media. It costs little to offer review copies of your CD as a digital download, your novel in an ebook format, or a sample of your performance on YouTube. Providing an online link to your reviewer materials can save you a significant chunk of change, both in production costs and postage.

Even in this digital age there are still some reviewers who will only review hard copy product. If they are important enough to your career, you should make those materials available to them as a 'on request' basis. From our experience as reviewers, sending out unsolicited hard copies of review product is a long shot gamble at best.

Folder

Put the contents of the press kit inside a two-pocket folder. There is no need to go crazy with high-end folders that have all kinds of bells & whistles. You don't have to buy expensive folders, but neither do you want to buy the 10-for-a-dollar folders from the local discount store during the back-to-school sale.

Sturdy black folders are the standard in the industry. If you want something more you can easily have a sticker of your latest project printed up. Artistically positioned on the front of your folder, it can make your press kit stand out from the dozens that entertainment reviewers receive each week.

Ancillary Promotional Materials

Although your press kit should be your primarily promotional focus, there are some ancillary materials that can help you as well.

Flyers

Before sending a journalist or potential show sponsor an expensive press kit, you can gauge their interest by sending them a flyer that describes your ministry, event or project. Be sure to include contact and booking information. Make a prominent note on the flyer that a full press kit is available upon request, and always include another copy of the flyer in your press kit.

We recognize that even a simply flyer can be expensive to produce and even more expensive to mail. You might want to consider building up your email list of fans, media and promoters and reaching out with an email blast rather than snail mail. There are tons of email clients that allow you to create dynamite electronic flyers. Many even provide invaluable feedback, including who opened your email, how many clicked on your links, who unsubscribed, etc. Mike and Paula use MadMimi.com for their email blasts, but we know people who are quite content with Constant Contact, MyEmma and others.

We've included on the next page a copy of a flyer Torry uses for his shameless self promotion.

TORRY MARTIN

An award-winning actor, author, screenwriter, and comedian who has delighted audiences for years with his zany personality and warm heart.

In addition to penning humor columns for a variety of national print and online publications including **Cloud Ten Pictures**, *On Course Magazine*, **Enrichment Journal**, and *Clubhouse Magazine*, Torry is the author of seven comedy sketchbooks published by **Lillenas Drama Publishers**. Martin's unique sense of humor caught the attention of the producers of Focus on the Family's popular children's audio series, *Adventures in Odyssey*, who enlisted him to lend his writing skills to the show. Torry went one step further, creating the delightful recurring character of **Wooton Bassett**.

An accomplished actor, Torry Martin starred in the national touring company of Columbia Artist's musical comedy, "Around the World in Eighty Days". He has appeared on **The Learning Channel** and the **Fine Living Network**, won top honors as both writer and actor in the **Nashville 48 Hour Film Project**, and has twice been named Grand Prize Winner for both Acting and Writing by the Gospel Music Association. A storyteller at heart, Martin has graced the stages of hundreds of secular and sacred venues across the country, sharing a brand of comedy described by Peabody Award-winning writer Paul McCusker as, "**Garrison Keillor with a spiritual perspective**."

Torry Martin has been a profiled in host of national and regional print and online publications including **Today's Christian**, *Light and Life*, *At Home Tennessee* and Christian-Movie.com. Martin is an in-demand speaker, performer and instructor at writing and filmmaking conferences across the U.S.

To learn more about Torry, please visit his website at www.torrymartin.com

Booking Information: **Torry Martin, P.O. Box 397, Sparta, TN 38583** tennesseetorry@yahoo.com | (865) 774-4444

Torry's flyer is short and sweet. It tells you who he is and what he does. It includes an endorsement from a respected and accomplished member of Torry's target market. It provides Torry's qualifications and drives readers to his website, i.e. ***"To learn more about Torry, please visit his website at www.TorryMartin.com."***

Note that in addition to his website, Torry includes his professional, not personal, contact information.

Postcards

Postcards are a quick, easy and relatively inexpensive way of putting your name, face or product in front of your target audience, and they have dozens of uses. You can send them in the mail as a follow up after sending a press kit to a media contact. You can send a postcard with a simple handwritten note as a thank you card to a promoter or journalist. Use them as leave-behinds after a personal appearance or as advanced promotion before an event. Their uses are limited only by your imagination.

There are plenty of low cost printers that can produce one or two-side postcards in either standard or over-sized dimensions. We've used VistaPrints.com and GotPrint.net, but there are many other quality printers out there. Shop around to get the best combination of quality, price and turnaround time.

Order postcards with a picture of yourself or your product on the one side. You can include a picture or additional info on the reverse, but if you want to send these postcards through the mail you'll need to leave room for an address.

Letterhead

Keep your correspondence professional in appearance. This means avoid sending out any promotional materials along with a note written on notebook paper. It looks cheap, because...well...it is cheap. Editors and DJs will immediately file it in the circular file. Instead, spend a few minutes creating simple letterhead.

You can do it yourself on your laptop and printer at home. It doesn't have to be, and probably shouldn't be, fancy. It just needs to look professional and provide your name and contact information in a font that is easy to read.

We've included below a copy of Paula's letterhead.

912 E. Lincoln St.
Tullahoma, TN 37388
paula@wordcrafts.net
www.wordcrafts.net

paula k parker

writing and creative services.....

Note the font is simple and easy to read. Her letterhead includes her name, contact information and, at the bottom of the page, a bit about what she does.

Labels

Print up labels with your name and contact information in a variety of sizes. You can have these professionally printed, or you can use your home computer and printer to do it yourself.

Stick these labels on your product. If you are a recording artist stick one on both your CD and on the jewel case. DJs are notorious for pulling the CD out of the case and then getting them mixed up with a bunch of other CDs so they may not be able to easily figure out who they are listening to or how to get into contact with you. Putting a label on your product will make their life easier, and might win you some brownie points with them.

Professional Packaging

As our photographer friend, Allen Clark, said earlier, "If a person had a good idea of what a good presentation for their photo was, nine times of out 10, their music sounded good. The bottom line is, when someone appears to know what they are doing, they probably do, and it translates across genres."

Allen is so right. A sharp looking press kit makes a huge impression. So does an amateurish press kit...but for all the wrong reasons. Continuity of your message is extremely important. Make sure your style and color scheme extends across your media platforms. If your CD cover is purple then make your press kit is purple.

An oft-observed faux pas to avoid like the plague: Make sure your press kit is free of hair - human/poodle/dog/cat etc. It happens, and it's gross. 'Nuff said.

Your press kit will likely be in a state of flux as you continue to update it with new press releases, new headshots and new product, so it doesn't make much sense to assemble hundreds of kits at a time. Instead, create a press box where you keep all of your press kit materials. Include files for headshots, tear sheets and product. When you need additional press kits, take your press box out of your closet, wipe your work surface down to make sure it is free of dust, dirt and that pesky pet hair, and assemble enough new press kits to meet your current needs. Then put your press box back into the closet where it is protected from the elements.

Chapter 3

The Basics of Publicity

Okay, you've got your press kit, business cards, flyers, and post cards. Now what? Now, it's time to start promoting yourself and your new book.

Come back here. Com'on! Trust us. This is not as scary as it might seem.

You're On Your Own, Kid

Regardless of whether you are a signed artist or an independent, nobody cares for your project as much as you do. Nobody should work as hard to promote it as you do. Even if your project is you.

If you are lucky enough to have the services of a professional publicist at your disposal, by all means, avail yourself of her expertise. Always keep her in the loop about stuff that is going on with your career that she can use. And never, EVER, do an end-run around her. Your publicist is paid to be your contact with the media. Let her do her job.

Having said that, if you are reading this book, chances are you don't have a publicist. But you don't have to wallow in self-pity and just hope something good happens to your career. In fact, there are some things you can do to promote yourself and your art without even having to contact a journalist.

Your Website

One would think that in this digital era, it should go without saying that every artist must have a website. Some artists, being artists, are so busy creating art that they don't take the time to create a website. Or if they have a website, they don't know how to promote their website. Remember what we said in the Prologue... wait; you did read the Prologue, didn't you? Well, in case you didn't, we said:

Creative people are often right-brained but, while the right-brain opens the door, it's the left-brain that does the business.

So, if you are one of those right-brained artists who does not have a website, we have two words for you - Get One.

Owning your own website looks more professional than the free, public ones and it gives you an air of legitimacy. Domain names are cheap, especially the ones that end with .me or .info – and web hosting doesn't have to cost an upper or lower extremity, either. Mike and Paula use GoDaddy to host their websites because this webhosting company is inexpensive and offers 24-hour customer service from real, live human beings who speak plain English. But since we don't have an endorsement deal with GoDaddy, our advice to you is to shop around for the best deal.

When it comes to selecting a name for your website, follow the advice of the Grail Knight from "Indiana Jones & The Last Crusade," "Choose - but choose wisely."

Choose a domain that people can easily identified with you, and make it easy to spell. Take into account that someone – hopefully *many someones* – will want to come to your website. If they can't spell it, they won't find it. A great example, or perhaps a really awful example, was the website for Mike's first novel. The book was entitled, "The Scavengers; Book One of The Tyrfingr Chronicles." His website was www.tyrfingrchronicles.com. It made perfect sense to Mike, because the book series was The Tyrfingr Chronicles, and he didn't want to have to create a new website for each subsequent book.

Paula thought it was a horrible domain name. She didn't think people would remember it, or even if they did, they wouldn't know how to spell it. "I had trouble finding the website," Paula explains. "Each time I wanted to visit it, I had to resort to either calling Mike into my office to ask how to spell it or just *Googling* his name, which presented its own problems since he has such a common name."

Study websites of people whose art is similar to yours. Make notes about what you like and what you don't like. Every website should have some basic sections, although you don't have to be bound by the same section names. You are a creative person, so feel free to get creative with the names, as long as you cover the bases.

Your **ABOUT** Section: This is where your Introduction goes. Some **ABOUT** sections have more than one page. The **ABOUT** section on Torry's website, www.torrymartin.com, includes a page for his **Bio**, **Photos**, **Quotes**, and a **Press** page with links to articles written about him.

Your **ART** Section: This is where information about what you do goes. You may have more than one **ART** section if you are involved in more than one aspect of the arts. Paula's website, www.paulakparker.com, has a separate **ART** Section for **Author**, **Playwright** and **Journalist**, while Torry's are listed as **Comedy**, **Writing**, **Acting** and **Networking**.

Your **NEWS** Section: This is where event information goes. You may have a calendar that lists your personal appearances here. You may use this section for press releases or other news items that concern you, such as a new product release or even celebratory personal events such as the birth of a new baby.

Your **STORE** Section: If your art involves a product, such as a book, CD or DVD, you can create an online store to help monetize your website. If you don't want the hassle of doing your own fulfillment [which really can devour a lot of your time] it is easy enough to join an affinity program with an online retain that carries your products, such as Amazon.com or ChristianBook.com. By linking to these sites you'll earn your royalties from your publishing company and get a referral bonus from the selling site as well.

Your **CONTACT US** Section: This is where you place your business contact information. As we have already said, and will probably say again, you need to protect your privacy. Never post your personal contact information on a public outlet such as your website. There are plenty of apps and plug-ins that will create a **CONTACT US** form that fans and potential clients can fill out. Add Captcha technology to help to reduce the spam. These programs will forward the contact query to your email so you can respond.

Your **BLOG** Section: This is where you write pretty much anything you want. We confess to not having a clue about the popularity of blogs. If "Shameless Self Promotion" had a blog we would blog about why we don't know why people read or write blogs. But let's face it, everybody and their dog has one. And the fact is...you need one, too.

Your **BLOG** helps your fans connect with you on a more personal level. Your fans become your friends, and your friends are better promoters than fans. Keep in mind that a blog is only valuable if you actually blog. If someone goes to your website and see that your blog hasn't been updated in months, they will assume you are either no longer in business, or that you don't care enough about your fans, friends, colleagues, or whatever, to stay in communication with them. They may think, *if he's not interested, why should I be interested?*

You *do* want them to be interested in you and your art, right?

Your **SHARE THIS** Button: Social networking is the marketing phenomenon of the decade. We'll talk more about social networking in a moment, so for now let's just say that your website should include **SHARE THIS** buttons on each page. Consider them digital Word-of-Mouth advertising.

Your **LINKS**: You know cool websites that you want to refer your friends to. This is a great place to do it. But this is a networking process, not a place to promote your favorite talking dog video. Make sure the sites you link to, are linking back to you. It is a double back-scratching process that benefits you both.

Social Networking

Five years ago, it was MySpace. Now it's Facebook and Twitter. Next week...who knows? Whether it's community from the comfort of your room, or constant communication with people who live miles, states, or even continents away from you, social networking sites are a phenomenon that you can't deny.

If you're an artist, you should regularly use social networking sites to promote yourself and your art.

"When my novel, "YHWH: The Flood, The Fish, and The Giant" was about to release, I began building my friend base on Facebook," Paula says. "That's not to say that I 'friended' every person on Facebook – some of those people are downright weird – but I did consistently check out people who were mutual friends of my existing Facebook friends and sent them a friend request. By the time the book released, I had over 1000 friends on Facebook. Now when I want to share news about my book, I post it as a note on my Facebook pages, which goes out to everyone who is a friend. And I know for a fact that some of my book sales came as a result of those notes."

A note of caution: Social networking can be one your greatest publicity tools, but it can also be the world's biggest time-waster. If you want to putter around on Facebook for a while, that's fine. Just don't confuse goofing off with working. Control the time you spend marketing on social media networking sites, or they will control your time.

The Media

How do you go about contacting the media to get publicity for your new film, book or public appearance? Before we get into that, it's probably important for you to understand the importance and influence of the media.

If you want to get the word out about your new CD, book, event, movie, play, political position, labor-saving device, or wondrous widget, you really only have three options: Word of Mouth, Advertising or Editorial.

Word of Mouth

Word of Mouth is probably the most effective - though perhaps the least controllable - means of getting your message to the masses. Back in the Seventies, there was a shampoo commercial that encouraged people to tell two friends about this wonderful product, and then they'd tell two friends, and so on, and so on. That ad agency had tapped into the world's most powerful and inexpensive marketing tool – Word of Mouth.

Think about it for a moment; who are you more likely to believe? A good friend who tells you how much they liked the newest Andrew Peterson CD or a slick magazine ad? Likewise, when someone whose opinion you highly respect tells you the latest Nicholas Cage flick stunk up the theatre, chances are you aren't going to plop down your hard earned bucks for a ticket and overpriced concessions to find out for yourself. Unless you happen to be a die-hard

Nicholas Cage fan... which Mike is... but we digress.

Movie studios spend untold thousands of dollars on free public screenings of upcoming movies. If their goal is to *sell* tickets, then why fill theaters across the country with unpaid backsides-in-seats?

Short answer - Word of Mouth. Major studios know how much it is worth.

Bragging rights for getting to see a movie for free and in advance of all your friends comes at a premium. If you've been to any of these pre-release screenings, you might find a studio representative standing outside the theater when you come out. She is looking for comments from those who saw the movie; and those comments will be taken seriously by the studio big-wigs. Hollywood is counting on everyone who sees the film - for free and in advance of the general release - bragging about it to all their friends; a much more cost-effective means of advertising than a :30 second trailer sandwiched between "Wheel of Fortune" and a rerun of "Law and Order."

Unfortunately, Word of Mouth is a slow build. It can also be difficult to generate, hard to control, and the least practical to measure.

Advertising

Advertising is another viable option. There is an old saying the ad industry; *You know what happens when you don't advertise? Nothing.*

When you advertise you have the advantage of being able to target your message as narrowly or as broadly as you choose. Advertising is a creative medium that can encompass everything from print to broadcast to cyberspace. You can hire a guy with an arrow sign to stand on the street corner, flipping and twirling it to hype your Friday night show. You can hire a skywriter to pen your message across the sky in letters a hundred feet tall.

Radio, cable television, newspapers, magazines – they'll all tell you why you should spend your advertising dollars with them. You can have your name and logo emblazoned on just about anything from bumper stickers to pencils, from t-shirts to billboards. You can advertise on the late, late show or on "Good Morning America"...*for a price.*

And therein - as the Immortal Bard intones - lies the rub; advertising always involves 'a price.'

In 2011, you could do a direct mail campaign utilizing a rented mailing list for a mere $875 per one thousand names. A full color, one-page ad in a popular Christian music magazine ran $6500. A spot during the 2008 Beijing Olympics began at three quarters of a million dollars. If you happen to have an extra $2.5 million lying around that you are not doing anything else with, the good folks at the Super Bowl would love to talk to you about purchasing :30 seconds worth of airtime.

The fact is, if you have enough money, you can advertise almost anywhere, on almost anything, even in space. Columbia Pictures once paid $50 grand to have "The Last Action Hero" graffitied onto the side of an unmanned rocket which was launched into space by the film's star, Arnold Schwarzenegger [of course, that didn't stop the movie from being one of the year's biggest box office flops]. Pregnant women have even auctioned off advertising rights to their bulging bellies on eBay. Torry says he tried that once...but didn't get any takers.

Like Word of Mouth, advertising is also an inexact science, yet it is possible to determine the effectiveness of at least some of your advertising. It's easy to track how many dollar-off coupons were redeemed for your latest project. It's not quite so easy to determine whether the customer who bought your latest book picked it up because they were intrigued by an ad in "Ladies Home Journal" or if it was a choice between that and another book they've already read at an airport newsstand. Maybe they were just a fan and would have bought the book whether or not they saw your ad. Who knows?

While carefully conceived, targeted, and executed advertising should certainly be a part of any marketing campaign, by its very nature, it has the stigma of being *paid for* by someone. Today's media savvy consumer takes most advertising with grain of salt. You know that no matter how great that famous super-model says the mascara is, in the back of your mind, you know someone paid her to say it. No matter how funny, cute, poignant or creative the ad, it doesn't mean it will compel anyone to actually buy your product.

"Life is pain, Princess," Wesley tells Buttercup in the classic film, "The Princess Bride." "Anyone who says different is *selling* something."

"I'm not a doctor, but I play one on TV..." Wow, we know that inspires *our* confidence in that product.

Editorial

Now, consider editorial content. By editorial, we're talking about feature articles, reviews, profiles, Question & Answer (Q & A's) in whatever medium you select – print, broadcast, or virtual. A thirty-minute interview can result in a one-page profile and, unlike advertising - which everyone expects to be chock full of hype - editorial content is generally expected to be at least relatively unbiased.

Think about a one-page feature in whatever magazine you can imagine; "Rolling Stone," "Billboard," "ParentLife," "Relevant," or "Christianity Today." Total impressions (the number of people impacted) is the same as a paid ad in that magazine. Total cost to you? Zero. Zip. Nada. Nothing [other than a half hour of your time].

Is a light bulb beginning to glow in the back of your brain? Same number of impressions? Higher credibility? Zero cost? Sound like a better idea?

You bet it does.

Of course, there are some drawbacks to generating editorial content. While every venue that carries advertising will be happy to take your money in exchange for one-sixth, one-third, one-quarter, one-half, or one full page to hype your project, getting one of their journalists interested in writing an article about you can present a bit of a challenge. Even if the journalist is your biggest fan, they still have to sell you to their editor. Let's face it; more people do an Internet Search for Casting Crowns than for the local Christian rock band that doesn't have a record deal.

There are things you can do to generate Word of Mouth.

You can give away CDs at your concerts. You can give free lectures at the local library. You can sponsor a free screening at the local theater. You can post a note about free MP3 downloads on your FaceBook page. You can energize your 'street team' with promises of free swag.

You can place advertising when and where you choose, assuming you have the budget to do so.

Editorial content, however, is self-selected and the self who is doing the selecting is not you. If someone is writing a story about you, it is because *they choose* to write a story about you.

Given the massive advantages of editorial content over just about any other form of promotional activity, doesn't it make sense to pursue it as portion of your marketing campaign? And, because the personal interview is the backbone of most editorial content, doesn't it make sense to learn how to give the best interview possible?

We'll give you a hint; the answer to both questions is 'Yes!'

Now before you pick up the phone or open an email to contact a media reviewer, you need to understand their needs.

Their Side of the Fence

There is a story that the two great writers, Ernest Hemingway and F. Scott Fitzgerald, were discussing their motivation for writing. Hemingway would only write when under the inspiration of his muse and would never allow pursing publication or earning money to influence his writing. Hemingway reportedly derided Fitzgerald, who had no problem studying his markets and writing for them. Fitzgerald was more interested in earning a living than writing the Great American Novel, although arguably, he did both.

So, what is the purpose of including this story in the chapter on publicity? Just this; before you contact a journalist or entertainment reviewer, you have to understand that these people are not writing the Great American Novel. At least they are not writing the Great American Novel about you. Like Fitzgerald, most of them are just trying to earn a living.

Or to quote Mike, the reason he writes entertainment-related articles is, "To make a buck." In case you think that sounds rather mercenary, let us make ourselves perfectly clear - it is, and we are.

Writing is what we do for a living. It pays our mortgage, puts food on our table, clothes on our backs, gas in our tank, and makes life a little easier. If we write a magazine article, it pays a bill. If we write a book, it continues to pay bills as long as people continue to buy the book. It's the old, 'Teach a man to fish...' syndrome.

If we had our way, we'd be sitting in a beautiful home office, on 100 acres of land, writing whatever struck our fancy that day, and live off the royalties of our Great American Novels. However, every day we walk into our smaller offices, sit down to our older computers and write what our editors – and ultimately our audience – want to read. Which might just be an article about you.

We've seen too many talented people completely blow an opportunity to get their message across, simply because they were unwilling or unable – through ego, pride, lack of sleep, nerves or lack of knowledge - to positively engage their interviewer.

The fact is, those of us in the media are only human. We would rather work with people who work with us than those who make our work harder. A great interview makes a great article. A difficult interview makes for a difficult article. A lousy interview generally won't even make it into print; at least as far as we are concerned. While we generally won't waste our time writing a negative article, that doesn't mean other journalists feel the same. Some journalists absolutely relish the opportunity to diss a project or artist. Unfortunately, some lousy interviews have ruined some people's careers and dramatically altered their lives.

The harsh reality is, not every guy with a microphone is willing to push beyond your monosyllabic answers to find out what you really mean. Not every woman with a tape recorder finds you as fascinating as you – or your mother - find yourself. Not every reporter with a steno pad cares about your mission, your passion, your project or even whether you live or die. There are some journalists out there who thrive on writing down-and-dirty-articles, who love to find a person's weakness – even if it's the inability to communicate who he is – and rip them to shreds in print.

We know of one particular singer who had an entire South American tour canceled because the tour sponsor read a scathing review in a popular magazine.

The Media gets a lot of flak from people, mostly from those who disagree with what they say. Journalists are often castigated as being liberal, pompous, and elitist; and those are just the nicer comments. Since Mike and Paula are part of the media, they are happy to correct that perception from their perspective.

"We are not liberal nor are we elitist and, to be honest, we are always surprised and humbled to learn that anyone reads what we write. That does not mean, however, that we do not realize the power of the media to promote – or harm – an artist's career," says Paula.

We dunno; maybe it's a power trip thing. Maybe they had a fight with their spouse before they left the house this morning. Maybe their shoes are too tight. Maybe, like the Grinch, their hearts are just two sizes too small. Bottom line is, while most journalists are really nice people, there are some downright nasty folks out there. Sadly, some of them are found in the Christian marketplace.

That is not how we approach an interview. We go into an interview with the idea that you have an interesting tale to tell and we want to help you tell it in such a way that someone wants to hear it. With that goal in mind, we've got a few questions we'd like to ask you. It would behoove you to know the answers to these questions before you talk to us - or to any other interviewer...

Why did you get into this business?
What's your story?
Why do you want to tell it?
Why should anybody care?

Remember, you want to end up in the human interest section, which everyone reads, rather than the religion section, which most people don't read. Not that we don't love the religion section, but...

If you followed our advice in Chapter One [which we know, as a smart person, you did] you will have already answered those questions. Regardless of how you've answered those questions, you need to realize *The Media* can help you with that.

Media List

One of the first things you need to do - even while you are scheduling a head shot photo shoot and hiring someone to write your bio – is begin building a media list. Start with magazines, newspapers, and websites you read on a regular basis. Check out the local radio and television stations and then do a Google search of different cities to get the names for their local stations.

Copy the names of their different writers as well as their mailing address, phone number and email address. Some of this information can be found on their company's website. Create a spreadsheet on your computer of these people and their contact information. You will use this list for sending out press releases.

Get as many as you can from each media site. You never know when someone might quit or move from one department to another.

Email Clients

You could copy and paste each email address from your media list into a separate email to send out individual press releases to every name on your list, but that would be way more time consuming that you can imagine, particularly if you have hundreds of names on your media list. There is an easier, and far more efficient, means of getting the word out. Use an email client.

There are tons of email clients out there, and yes, they all cost money. Trust us, it is money well spent, just in the time it will save you. Popular email clients include Mad Mimi, Constant Contact and MyEmma. Do a Google search and you'll find plenty more.

With an email client you can maintain, organize and sort your mailing lists. You can control when your emails are sent and who receives them. Email clients will even tell you who opened your email and whether they clicked on any web links you may have included with your press release.

Email clients charge a fee, which varies according to the level of service you sign up for. Shop around until you find the deal that works best for you.

Press Releases

A press release is a vital part of publicizing your book/CD/film/event, yet so many people overlook this very simple but most effective tool. If you seriously feel that you can't write your own press release or you just feel awkward about it, welcome to the club. Torry didn't want to write his first press release.

"I went to the local newspaper and hired a reporter for $20 to write one for me," Torry explains. I presented him with all of the information that I thought needed to be in the article and left the rest to him. The result was a polished press release that I was very pleased with and got a lot of results from. I sent that first press release to four different newspapers and two television news stations and they all ran the story."

Every press release involves the standard who, what, where, when, why and how. For those of you who feel comfortable writing your own press releases, here are some helpful hints.

The Essentials of Press Releases

1) Always use your letterhead for your press releases. This applies whether you are sending out a hard copy or using an email client to deliver your press release. Use a standard type font, like Times New Roman or Courier. A press release is not the place to get fancy. Your target audience just wants to be able to read what you have to say without having to work at it.

2) Always date your press release to indicate when the information should go live. If you want the information to hit the news immediately, the first line should state, in all caps, FOR IMMEDIATE RELEASE. If the information needs to be held for a later date, the first line should state FOR RELEASE OCTOBER 23 (or whatever date you want the information published).

3) Always include a catchy headline, centered and in all caps. Beneath the headline you may include a descriptive sentence to further entice your reader.

4) Always start the body of your press release with a date line that includes the city, state and date, followed by a dash, then start your press release (Nashville, TN, August 12, 2010 - WordCrafts Press announced the release of...)

5) Always use the body of the press release to answer the *who*, *what*, *where*, *when*, *why* and *how* that every journalist wants to know.

6) Appeal to authority. Although it is not absolutely required, including a quote or accolade from an influential individual adds credibility to your work.

7) Always include the standard FOR MORE INFORMATION line at the bottom of your press release, followed by the name and contact information of the person who can provide more information. You can use this to direct readers to your website, to note that you are available for interviews, or to note that review copies of your project or high resolute photos are available upon request.

Keep your press release short and to the point. One page is ideal. More than two pages goes from newsworthy to snooze-worthy. Keep in mind that journalists get bombarded with press releases. If you don't capture their interest in the first couple of sentences, your press release will likely end up in the circular file.

"Trust us on this," Mike says. "Paula and I receive on average over 50 press releases a day. We hit 'delete' more often than we read the press releases."

We've included a copy of the press release announcing the U.S. release of Paula's book, "YHWH: The Flood, The Fish & The Giant."

FOR IMMEDIATE RELEASE

THE FLOOD, THE FISH & THE GIANT SEES U.S. RELEASE

Ancient Mysteries Retold Series Celebrates 400th Anniversary of the King James Bible.

Nashville, TN – June 1, 2010 – YHWH: The Flood, The Fish & The Giant, published by Authentic Media and released in the United Kingdom last month, arrived on American shores on June 1st. The book is a collection of classic, ancient tales from the Old Testament, retold in a fresh and vibrant way for a generation that is perhaps more familiar with Hogwarts and Olympus than the Garden of Eden.

A number of major chain bookstores in the U.K. have shown a marked reluctance to stock the book due to the monotheistic symbolism contained in the ancient stories. The publisher noted that it was not uncommon for secular U.K. bookshops to only stock a limited number of what they perceive as Christian titles, believing them to have limited appeal to a minority market. YHWH: The Flood, The Fish & The Giant does not appear to be facing that same issue in the United States as the book has already been embraced by such chains as Barnes & Noble, Parable Christian Stores, Lemstone Stores, Amazon and many others.

In addition to experiencing growing acceptance at retail, the book is finding fans from Nashville to Hollywood and all points in between.

Popular Christian recording artist and author, Bonnie Keen (First Call), commented, "Mega kudos to Paula Parker and G. P. Taylor for bringing this fresh collection of timeless adventures to a new generation. As one often hears, 'You can't make this stuff up!' YHWH: The Flood, The Fish & The Giant fits the bill for any reader longing to embrace a heart-pounding story where the underdog wins the day and good triumphs against all odds over evil. In this marvelous new work we remember afresh why Biblical stories have infiltrated centuries of literature, culture and most importantly continue to capture the human heart."

Filmmaker, Mitchell Galin (Stephen King's 'The Langoliers') added, "What an absolute delight. Rarely have I seen stories so vividly portrayed; portrayed in a way that makes them come alive the way a good campfire story comes alive. And the source, the greatest stories ever told, but in a way that makes them accessible as they have not been before. You can walk through the gardens, feel Noah's confusion, experience Abraham's anguish, but in all we see unquestioned faith. We've heard or read the stories before, but what G.P.Taylor and Paula K. Parker have done is make you "feel" the stories in a new profound way."

"I know many young people and adults who don't read the Bible simply because they don't think the language is understandable," says co-writer, Paula K. Parker. "YHWH: The Flood, The Fish & The Giant presents these ancient stories from a fresh perspective in order to appeal to contemporary readers who are fans of Harry Potter and Percy Jackson."

"The purpose of the book is not to proselytize or convert," adds co-author G.P. Taylor, a New York Times Bestselling author, "but to give children, young people and adults a taste of the mystery of one of the most life changing books ever written. It is an introduction to the stories that have entertained and thrilled people for thousands of years.

"2011is the 400th anniversary of the King James version of the Bible," Taylor continues. "Much of our language is rooted in that book. Sadly, we are in the position that within a generation the understanding of the book that underpins our language could be gone forever."

YHWH: The Flood, The Fish & The Giant is distributed in the United States by STL Distribution. For a preview visit YHWHbook.com.

Fans can stay current with the book at facebook.com/YHWHBOOK.
For more information about Authentic Media visit AuthenticMedia.co.uk
For more information about Paula K. Parker visit PaulaKParker.com
For more information about GP Taylor visit GPTaylor.info

Using the Press Release

When writing and servicing press releases there are some things to keep in mind, not the least of which is knowing what type of media you are engaging - print, broadcast or online.

First and foremost, your press release has to be newsworthy. The media's advertising department will print just about anything you write as long as you are paying for it, but if you are looking for coverage in the Entertainment or Lifestyle section, you've got to make your press release sound more like news and less like an ad. To do this you've got to provide the journalist or editor with a reason to run your story. Show them how your story can impact their community or industry.

The best press release in the world will not do you one speck of good unless you send it to the right media. A story about your work with an organization that rescues baby squirrels might work well for a nature magazine, or even as a human interest feature in your local newspaper, but it probably wouldn't generate much interest from a financial investments website.

Freelance writers study the markets to find magazines, journals, newspapers, podcasts and websites that run the kinds of stories they write. You need to do the same thing. Otherwise you are just scattering your seed on rocky ground and hoping the birds don't carry it off - which they probably will.

Write your press release from a journalist's perspective. A properly formatted press release about a timely story with a newsworthy angle is a dream come true for most journalists. If you can make their lives easier they are far more likely to run your story.

When it comes to comedy and press releases, timing is everything. A great press release does you no good if you miss the outlet's deadline. Online publications may have the editorial flexibility to get a press release in the morning and have it online the same day. Some print publications, however, have their stories planned out six month in advance or even longer. When in doubt, ask.

Freelancers frequently request a copy of their target publication's editorial calendar so they can pitch story ideas that will match. You can do the same thing. Find ways to fit into the publication's theme issue, whether it is your participation in a political rally for an election day theme, or your volunteer work with Habitat for Humanity for a charity-themed issue.

Food for Thought: Your participation in events that are connected to charities is newsworthy. As believers, it is a good thing to participate in and to support charitable events, but be sure to check to the motives of your heart. If you do it just to get your name in the paper…verily, verily you have your reward.

Follow Up

You built your media list, wrote a great press release and serviced it through an email client. Now you can just sit back and wait for the calls for interview requests to come pouring in, right?

Do we really have to say, "Wrong?" Of course not.

"We really do get hundreds of press releases each week," Paula insists. "I promise you, we are *not* exaggerating. If anything, we're understating the amount. We open only a handful of those emails. One thing that makes us think about pursuing a possible story is follow-up. It's not that we are not interested, we just don't have the time to write something about every press release that comes across our email. When we get a phone call or email from the publicist reminding us of the press release we are much more likely to revisit it."

Make sure the press releases you send out are newsworthy, send them out regularly and follow up in a timely manner. Just don't be a pest about it. Nobody likes that irritating child tugging at your shirt and saying, "Hey, hey, hey, hey, hey..."

Talking to Editors and Reporters

You got a great story to tell. You've sent out a killer press release, and you are getting some response. A reporter wants to interview you to get some additional information for a piece in Sunday's paper.

To quote Han Solo, *'Great, kid! Don't get cocky.'*

You had all the time in the world to craft a great press release. You may only have a few minutes on the phone to get your message across to a reporter, so it is important to know what you want to convey before the questions get asked.

When the reporter calls, be friendly. Answer her questions but be sure to interject the information you want them to use. The reporter might be writing as they talk to you.

Be prepared to give additional details and quotes. The more specific and anecdotal you are, the more your remarks will be quoted. Be as detailed as possible. You don't want to sound like you are reading a script, but you don't want to get your information wrong either. If there are facts and figures involved, write them down so you can refer to them.

If you have never been interviewed by a reporter before, it can be a nerve-wracking experience.

"I've interviewed hundreds of people over the years, ranging from everyday housewives to Oscar Award winning film directors," says Mike. "I wasn't nervous interviewing Pierce Brosnan or Sir Ridley Scott, but put me on the other side of the microphone, and somehow I get tongue-tied and my mouth goes dry."

Rehearse beforehand by having a friend, colleague or your spouse ask you questions based on your press release. Have her throw in a couple of zingers that you don't expect, just to see how you respond to them. Rehearsing your answers will help you appear clever and witty when the real questions are asked. Key in on exactly what the reporter wants, so you can target your answers around the story's angle.

Offer to meet the reporter for lunch or coffee. Meet him at a place that is convenient for him. Let the reporter know if you have appropriate photos that can accompany the story.

Radio Publicity

Ah, radio. What would we do without it? People spend a lot of time in their vehicles - commuting to work, traveling, shopping or just killing time. Some studies indicate the average person spends two hours a day in a car. You have a captive audience and therefore the *perfect* audience. While getting your information on the air is similar to print or internet media, there are some things distinctive to radio.

U B U

Each radio station is unique, at least in their own minds. When you send out a press kit you will increase your chances for exposure by finding something unique and including it with your press kit. This is one time it is perfectly okay to be a little outside the box, even leaning toward the unusual or bizarre.

"It's all in the content and the presentation," declares our friend, Larry Wayne, on-air personality for the K-LOVE radio network. "If your product, service, or position on an issue is in line with the demographics of the station that you're contacting, and if the presenter [that's *YOU!*] is tight, bright and brief – not to mention compelling – then you are showing a lot of green flags!"

Think outside the box and make it fun. Drop by the morning shows at a local station and ask if you can hang out with the DJs. Talk to the producer. Ask if you can have your band on the air on a Friday. Write an event-specific jingle for the station as a freebie. There is always a reason for a radio station to have a party. Offer to give a free concert to the tenth caller. You're a creative person, right? This is the time to let your creativity run wild.

Network stations can present greater challenges than locally owned stations, but that is no reason to avoid them.

"There are probably more management layers in a network

situation, but I'd really just try to contact individual air talent in either situation," Larry notes. "They generally hold a lot of sway with bosses in terms of getting you on the air."

Larry also has some advice about the best way to get your press information to radio personalities. "We all live on email these days," Larry says. "No snail mail, unless you are sending a book or something, and absolutely no faxes."

Never – *ever* – go to the advertising people unless you specifically and intentionally want to buy advertising. It's not that we don't like advertising people. We're sure they are very nice and have lovely families. But their job is to convince you to pay them money. Your job is to get publicity, which does not involve paying them money.

"If you don't want to pay for an ad then never – *ever* – go to the advertising people," Torry reiterates. "If you were in one of my workshops you would hear me repeat this at least four times, so consider this warning repeated thricely."

GiveAways

Radio loves giveaways. It provides added value to their listeners. You know, *'We are giving away free tickets to...fill in the blank...to the 16th caller...'* If you're going to be interviewed on the radio, it is a great idea to put together a giveaway pack. When Paula was interviewed over the radio for "YHWH: The Flood The Fish and The Giant," she made sure there were copies of the book for the DJ to give away on the air.

The DJ may use the giveaway to tease the audience several times within their on-air time before they actually give your product away. How cool is that? It's like you have a mini-ad for your CD six times in an hour, and you didn't pay a dime for it! The listener wins, because she gets a free goodie. The station wins because they look like good guys for giving stuff away. And you win because you have just increased your visibility exponentially for minimal cost. We're pretty sure the cost of the product you gave away was far less than the cost of buying a :30 second ad.

Put together a giveaway pack that is unique. Remember, UBU. It might be two tickets to your upcoming concert or a copy of your book, but you can make it more appealing if it more than just about you. Is your book a Christmas book? Go to the after Christmas sales and buy a bunch of ornaments or Christmas coffee mugs that are 75% off. Put together a package kit that you can give away during your promotional events next Christmas. If your novel is a romance, go out the day after Valentine's Day and stock up on heart-shaped cookie cutters, etc..

If your giveaway involves tickets, *never* mention the price of the tickets, because the price might change. Even if the event is free, just say, "I'm speaking at the civic center this Friday and we're giving away two free tickets."

"When I am going to be somewhere, I go to Christian Book Distributors, find out what Adventures in Odyssey products they have that are 75% off right now," says Torry. "I order 10 to 12 of those, get a VeggieTales DVD, add some Alaskan stuffed animals and make it a fun give away package. Now the radio DJ has something to talk about; it sounds really big, but it didn't cost me a lot of money."

Give Away Thoughts

Perhaps your church is presenting a Christmas cantata. Ask members of the congregation who might also be business owners to donate items for giveaways. Restaurant owners may donate a dinner for two; car wash owners might donate a free car wash. Free tickets to the event that DJs can give away on the air are always a hit.

Even if the cantata is free and open to the public, printed tickets provide an air of legitimacy. Print up some tickets to give them away. Paper clip the tickets to a concert flyer that includes pertinent information about you and the concert.

Always give the tickets out in pairs. We mean, really, who wants to go to an event alone?

DJs love to give stuff away to their listeners, but DJs are people, too. They like free stuff as much as the next guy. In addition to a giveaway package for listeners, take something for the DJ. Just make sure whatever you take is store-bought, not homemade.

It's not that your oatmeal cookies aren't the best of the best, but the DJ doesn't know you from Adam - except that Adam is probably a lot older than you. And for all you know the DJ might be allergic to oatmeal. Instead, take her a bag of fresh coffee and a coffee mug. Donuts or bagels from the local bakery are always a hit with radio folks.

Bring along extra tickets of your upcoming performance that are just for the on-air staff in addition to those that are used as promotional listener giveaways.

"Okay, so I have this cool giveaway package," you say. "How

do I convince the radio guy that it's cool and he should give it away?"

"It doesn't take any convincing," Torry explains. "Most of the time if you tell them it's a giveaway, they will love it. The thing about radio is that you have to be *exclusive* with that station. If you go to another station in the same market with the same giveaway, neither one of them is going to do it. Radio stations are gratified when you say, *'Hey, we've chosen you! You're our favorite radio station, yada, yada, yada.'* If you want to gain traction with a radio station, you've got to build a relationship with the people at that radio station."

Torry started his writing career by creating three characters - Granny Glockenspiel, Judge Mental and Bob the Highway Guy. They were radio call-in characters for a radio sketch. Torry wrote the script for local radio stations. The DJ would call him once a month to record four episodes. Once a week, Granny would "call in" and interact with the DJ. Torry only provided the sketches and interaction to one station in a market.

If you're a musician, consider writing a parody of a seasonal holiday song that incorporates the DJ or the local radio station. Record it and give to the radio station. Radio prefers to work in trade and may reciprocate.

"Whenever I went to a different town, I would tweak the radio spot for the specific station's use," says Torry. "I've had stations cut professional commercials for my bookings as a result."

So, What About Radio Advertising?

I know, I know; we mentioned at the beginning of the book that people take advertising with a grain of salt, realizing that someone paid for those wonderful things to be said about their product. But there is a reason that companies keep paying for advertisements - because they work! To answer some of the questions concerning radio advertisements, we turned to our friend, Larry Wayne.

Shameless Question: How expensive – and difficult – is it to get a good radio ad produced?

Larry Wayne: As the saying goes, most of the time you get what you pay for. I'm not saying you can't produce a great ad on a shoestring budget. Computer technology has made it possible for great radio ads to be made in someone's home rather than in an expensive studio. I am saying that just because someone offers you their services at a discount doesn't mean you should take his low-ball rate.

When a company or individual gives you an offer, do your homework. Ask to hear some of the stuff he has produced. Talk to others who have worked with this person. Your ad is often the way the public will perceive you. You only get one chance to make a good first impression.

Shameless Question: How could a person on a limited budget get a commercial made?

Larry Wayne: Very often the radio station you are placing your ads on will offer to produce the ad for free. This may or not be a bargain, depending on the quality of their production. Again, you need to do your homework.

Shameless Question: Okay, so my ad is produced. What should I expect to pay to have it run on air?

Larry Wayne: This depends on too many things to even give you a ballpark figure. Rating of the station, size of the market, time of day, and other factors contribute to the price. In a soft economy, most stations will negotiate on fees.

Other Radio Promotion Ideas

Radio is all about ratings, and clever stunts can help generate audience. A bungee jumping Stunt Angel will certainly generate publicity for your Christmas cantata - as long as you are properly insured. The more outlandish the better; as long as it fits the station's format and isn't immoral or illegal, almost anything goes.

The most important thing to remember about dealing with radio stations is to simply be their friends and shower them with gifts.

If you are a Christian rock band, you've got a great opportunity with the local college station. Chances are they will play your music because they are always looking for a fresh new sound. Of course, if the local college is not a Christian college you'll need to avoid the Christian lingo that is familiar to believers, but may be nearly incomprehensible to many in the mainstream. Be approachable and fun. Concentrate on the _music_ rather than the _lyrics_. Once they are playing your music, the message will take care of itself and you can put the airplay on your resume.

College stations are not the only place indie artists can get airplay. Even major network stations may be open to playing your music...if your music meets their needs.

"With the entire music industry changing so much, the tradition of stations only playing artists who are on a recognized label is pretty much a thing of the past," says Larry Wayne. "Although I am not the one who makes music decisions – or even listens to new music for possible adds – my feeling is that it's all about your sound and your message. You stand a better chance of getting your music on the radio if it's professional, hip and happening, and it fits the format, than you do if you recorded and produced your song in your basement."

Chapter Four

The Interview

Before talking about how *you* prepare for an interview as the interviewee, we thought it might help to let Mike explain how he and Paula prepare for an interview as the interviewers – to let you see the process from the far side of the microphone.

As we mentioned earlier, part of the reason we write is to earn a living. But money is not our only motivation. There is an additional reason for why we do what we do; we desire to promote the Kingdom of God through our writing. We consider it to be a divine appointment, and we take it very seriously.

We pray before every interview because we believe our meeting whoever we are interviewing can be a ministry moment. We believe that the stories we write about people and their art can impact the reader, in much the same way great music impacts the listener, and a great stage performance can impact the theatre-goer. Our responsibility is to help the person we are interviewing to tell their story in such a way that it might minister to the people who read it.

Setting up the Interview

When you write for a living, you discover that you are everybody's best friend, particularly people who want to get their message out to the people who read what you write. Like many facets of life, while 'what you know' is vitally important, many times 'who you know' is actually the thing that pushes the final button.

There is no shortage of people who want to be interviewed. That's where a good publicist/PR person comes into play. For us, writing a profile or feature article begins with contacting the artist's/author's/actor's publicist to schedule an interview. Or more likely, having the publicist contact us to suggest an interview with their client.

We rarely contact the person we want to interview directly, unless they don't have a publicist or PR person who handles their calendar. Over the years we have developed personal friendships with a number of "celebrities," particularly in the Christian entertainment industry, and while we know they would be happy to talk to us directly, there are industry protocols that need to be observed. Whenever possible, we always go through the proper channels. Trust us – no one likes to be circumvented.

There are several things we mention when requesting an interview.

The first is the publication or website we are writing the article for. This is important information for the artist to know, because different media outlets have different slants, particular if it is a denominational publication. You don't want to step on religious toes if you can keep from it. It is easier for us to discuss any possible editorial slants before actually conducting the interview.

We generally have an idea of what direction we want our article to take before the interview. Maybe the artist has a new CD/book/movie and we want to write an article about that. Maybe they just a life-changing experience we want to explore. Sometimes a whole different article emerges from chasing bunny trails that come up during the interview.

Back in 2002, we spoke to many artists who had been involved in the 9/11 relief efforts. In 2005, we spoke to artists who had gone to Louisiana and Mississippi after Hurricane Katrina. Paula interviewed the Steven Curtis Chapman family about their support of adoption and their personal adoptions of three little girls from China. She interviewed the real Sean and Leigh Anne Touhy about the movie, "The Blind Side." She spoke with Jeremy Camp about the loss of his first wife to cancer, and with Sandy Patti about her weight loss. Mike chatted with Natalie Grant about her Home Foundation that is battling the scourge of human trafficking.

If the publication we are writing for has a list of topics they want covered in the article, we'll email them to the artist. We've found that letting the artist know the direction of the interview in advance helps them prepare better answers to our questions.

There are dozens of details involved in setting up an

interview. Stuff like the article's deadline, the writer's lead time, when the writer is available, when the artist is available, how much time we'll need for the interview, and whether it will be done in person, over the phone, or even via email.

We always prefer in-person interviews. It's may be easier to arrange a telephone interview, but you just get so much more out of it when you talk to a human face-to-face. And there are certain nuances that you don't catch in any other medium. If you are going to do an in-person interview, there is the issue of where to meet.

Lot's of PR people and artists love to meet at Starbucks or some other equally cool coffee shop. Now, we are not dissing Starbuck, or any other equally cool coffee shop. The fact is, we love great coffee and we love the ambiance. But a coffee shop is really not the ideal choice for us to conduct an interview.

Why?

Because we record our interviews. And regardless of how great our recording devices are, the sound of the coffee-grinder suddenly crushing a pound of Jamaican Blue Mountain, or the hissing and sputtering of the cappuccino-machine in the background can drown out that incredibly insightful answer the artist just gave us.

Finding a nice, quiet location is something we always try to work out when scheduling an in-person interview.

As much as we enjoy eyeball-to-eyeball interviews, sometimes they are just not always possible. Sometimes time and geographical considerations take precedence and we have to schedule a telephone or Skype interview. In those instances, we arrange who will place the call, make sure we [or they] have the correct phone number, and double-check the artist's time-zone if it is different from ours. You'd be amazed at how confusing time zones can be, particularly if Daylight Savings Time is involved.

We try to confirm our interview information via email and copy all parties involved. This way, everyone has a copy of the scheduled interview and mistakes can be corrected ahead of time. We also give them the url for our website. This allows the artist the opportunity to learn something about us and our writing style before the interview.

We try to check back with them the day before the interview, just to make sure everything is still a go. Let's face it, life happens. Sometimes even when you have an interview scheduled another situation arises that takes precedence. And sometimes someone just forgets about the interview, or failed to note it on their calendar. An email on the day before serves as a friendly reminder and helps to minimize foul ups.

Research and Prep

"Remember when we mentioned that we receive dozens of press releases, along with CD, galleys of books, press releases, DVDs, movie screeners, etc. each week?" Paula asks. "Most of the time, we will have the background information we need on the person we are about to interview. Occasionally, we don't. In those cases we'll ask for one to be sent.

"We'll read the press material, listen to the CD, read the book, or screen the movie prior to the interview. We might do other research, such as talking to the producers, label execs, ministry partners, or just perusing the web for additional background information.

"During all of this preparation, we make notes about things that we might want to ask during the interview. We have our questions handy during the interview, but if something interesting in the conversation captures our attention, there is no telling what bunny trail we might decide to chase."

Learning To Serve

Jesus once told His disciples that in order to be great, you must first learn to serve. The same admonition is true in virtually every area of life. *"Thanks for the sermon, preacher, but how does that apply to me getting some free publicity?"* Glad you asked.

Of course, the feature article is all about you, but getting it written is all about us. As professional writers, Mike and Paula can tell you first hand that if you make our lives easier, they'll love you forever. Here's a hint - Mike and Paula are not so very different from every other journalist out there.

Interviewers are always looking for a new angle. "Help us out and we'll be your friend for life," Mike says. "Give us a fresh angle on why we're doing this interview and we'll give you a fresh feature article, rather than a rehash of the same article with the same pat answers you'll see in six other magazines."

In other words, learn to serve your interviewer.

Perhaps you are an actor. Do you support a particular cause other than your upcoming film? Is there something about your character in this film that touched a personal spot in your life? Maybe you are an author. Is there an interesting story behind why you wrote a Christian mystery? Perhaps you are a musician. Is there a reason for us to talk to you that does not have to do with the music? Does a particular song have a special story behind it?

For over twenty years, Gospel Music Association (GMA) Week was held in Nashville, Tennessee, every April. GMA was a week-long opportunity for Christian artists, both new and established, to see and be seen by the movers and shakers in the industry, the gatekeepers, the media and, of course, the fans.

For fifteen consecutive years Mike and Paula attended GMA Week. The interviews came fast and furious. "One year, we talked to forty-some-odd artists over a three-day stretch," Mike recalls. "Some of those artists were old friends we wanted to catch up with. Some we already had assignments to write stories about. Most of the artists we interviewed we do not know beforehand and had no prior assignment to write a story about. We interviewed these artists because we had a relationship with their publicist. As you can imagine, by the time the week was over, our brains were fried. "

Even more daunting than the GMA interview feeding frenzy was the task of transcribing the mind-numbing array of those recorded conversations – a task that takes much longer than the interviews.

"In the weeks following GMA, the artists we have assignments to write about were the recordings that got transcribed first," Paula explains. "After that, it was the ones that left us intrigued - the ones that left us wishing we had been able to spend more time with the artist - that wormed their way into our writing schedule. These were the ones we'd take to our editors as ideas for future articles."

During one such GMA Week, they did a routine interview with the rock band, Holland. Here's an excerpt from the article Mike wrote about them for "Living With Teenagers" magazine:

Will Holland looks like a rock star - tall, wiry, intense - with soulful eyes and a mournful voice, sheathed in faded blue jeans and a black t-shirt. He commands the stage as he fronts the band that bares his name, performing a satisfying blend of rebellion and reminiscence; youthful exuberance and world-weary cynicism; hooky, can't-get-it-out-of-your-head melodies and moody, angst-ridden lyrics. In short, Will Holland plays rock 'n' roll that is custom-made for the hormone-charged teenage years. That is understandable since he is barely out of his teens.

Juxtaposed against Will's on-stage persona is the quiet, soft-spoken, thoughtful poet that inhabits his clothes when he is out of the limelight. The poet and the rock star join forces in Holland's achingly honest debut project, "Photographs and Tidalwaves."

"I always want to have a real honest approach to songwriting, to be vulnerable, because I think people can connect with that more easily," Will explains. "We moved to Nashville right after I graduated from high school because we had to start writing for our new album, but about a month before we moved one of my best friends got killed in a car accident. It was a real hard thing. The songs I wrote for the album had a lot to do with things I was going through at the time – moving away from home, Jim's death, my girlfriend breaking up with me. There were a lot of changes. That's real life."

Though Will was a Christian (as was his friend, Jim), he says that event shook him to his core. He credits his parents with helping him deal with his grief and get on with life.

"The best thing my parents did during this time was just to be there for me," he says. "And to make sure that I knew they were there. They didn't necessarily tell me how to feel about it or send me to counseling or anything. They just listened."

> *- from "A Grief Observed," first published in* "Living With Teenagers Magazine"

A youthful, soft-spoken, poet/rock star touched us with his story of the death of a friend, and how it impacted him. He told of the songs he wrote to help him get through that very tough time. His story was unique, yet universal; and that was exactly what made it so important!

Death is a part of life. Adults come to accept that inevitability as they watch the previous generation die off, one by one. But teenagers process death differently - it was obvious in Will Holland's answers, in his body language, in the far-off, haunted look in his eyes. Mike pitched the idea to "Living With Teenagers" magazine, and instead of a short blurb on just another rock band, Holland got a three page spread with a CD review as a sidebar in a major magazine targeting parents of teens.

You can't buy that kind of publicity.

It happened because Will Holland was willing to share a story from his personal experience that impacted him deeply. He was willing to serve us by giving us something that wasn't just about selling albums, but was about helping parents learn how to help their children deal with grief.

Remember, people are looking for answers, not just information and entertainment. Helping them solve their problems in life - kids, marriage, finances, etc. - will help you broaden your platform.

The Pre-Interview

You're in a classroom. Worse... you don't know what subject is being taught in this classroom. Worse still... you suddenly realize a test is being given today that you haven't studied for... and you're in your underwear. And your mother hasn't washed them.

Ever had a dream like that? Do you remember the gut-wrenching, heart-palpitating panic? And the relief when you woke up?

Going into an interview unprepared is like living that dream. Stop and think about it for a minute – you are about to be in front of someone you may never have met, who is going to record everything you say or do, and they are going to share their slant on your conversation with the whole world, or at least their little part of it.

Scary? Yeah. It can be.

So what are you going to do about it? Our friend, publicist Melissa Campbell Goodson, has this suggestion:

"Do Your Homework!"

We know; you thought you left that behind when you graduated from high school. You may not have been one of those students who loved doing homework – and we're not even sure a person like that exists – but good students will tell you, that's how they earned those high marks. Good interviews are a result of both the interviewer and the interviewee doing their homework.

Since we've discussed what we, as interviewers, do to

prepare for an interview, it's time to look at what you, as a potential interviewee, should do to get ready.

"If the interview will be extensive - for instance, a cover story interview might require several hours of interview time - do your homework on the interviewer, reading as many background articles and features (written by the interviewer) as you can find," Melissa Campbell Goodson tells her artists. "Use your publicist to find out a little about them. Hopefully, they will do their homework, too."

Melissa is 100 percent right, regardless of whether it is an extensive interview or a short meet and greet. Learning what you can about your interviewer can pay huge dividends. You might find some common ground between the two of you that puts you both at ease and forms the basis of a new relationship, or that spins the interview in a totally unexpected direction. Perhaps you are both Elvis fanatics. Taking a few moments to discuss your visit to Graceland can help to break the ice.

Are you and your interviewer from Texas? Instant affinity! Conversely, if you are a dyed-in-the-wool Republican and you discover the guy doing the interview is a yellow-dog Democrat, you know you want to stay away from discussing politics. Unless, of course, your new book is on the history of politics or you were asked to sing at the Republican National Convention. Even so, at least you know there are some potential areas of conflict that you'll want to tread carefully around.

How do you find out stuff about your interviewer? Check to see if they have a website. Whenever Mike and Paula interview someone who has gone to their website to read about them, it makes a *huge* impression.

"A few years back, during Gospel Music Week in Nashville, Paula and I had an interview schedule with a relatively unknown rock-worship artist named Todd Agnew," Mike recalls. "I had previously reviewed his debut major label project, "Grace Like Rain," for a major industry publication, but the release date got pushed back and practically everyone had forgotten about it.

"When we met, Todd mentioned that review and how he felt like it really captured what he was trying to say. He went on to say he had Googled us and found out quite a bit about the kinds of things we wrote."

Were we impressed? Oh, yeah.

Are we fans for life? Oh, yeah.

Do we go out of our way to find ways to write about Todd? You betcha. Because now it's no longer a 'what can you do for me,' situation, but a two-way conversation. We weren't the only ones Todd had researched, by the way; every writer friend we know who interviewed Todd that year had the same experience.

Now, we're not saying Todd's rise to the top of the charts had anything to do with his ability to connect as effectively with his interviewers as he does with his fans, but... well, yes, maybe we are saying that. At the very least, it didn't hurt.

It is entirely possible that there is no background information available on the person who will be conducting your interview, or there may be no time to do research. Your first line of defense is your publicist. Part of the publicist's job is to know something about the interviewer.

If your publicist doesn't know anything about the interviewer, she should at least know something about the publication or media outlet the interview is for.

Our friend, Dennis Disney of D-Squared Entertainment confirmed our suspicions that *proper prior preparation prevents pitifully poor performances.* And as he so eloquently notes, your performance reflects on more than just you.

"The person being interviewed must do his/her own homework on who the publication/media outlet is and what the purpose of the interview is," Dennis insists. "In other words, the interviewee should do some brief homework or at least be well briefed by the publicist/manager/agent."

Dennis recalled an example of an in-office presentation at "Billboard Magazine," which was coordinated for one of his clients by a well-respected Nashville-based publicist. Everyone involved was pumped! This was "Billboard Magazine" - the Big Boy On The Block, the Big Man On Campus, the Big Kahuna, the Head Honcho, the Bible of the Music Industry. It is not every day you get the chance to rub shoulders in that heady atmosphere.

"The presentation was going well with about twenty editorial staffers in the Billboard conference room," Dennis explained. "My client was doing a great job of sharing her story, and then began sharing her conversion to Christianity, explaining her faith, just a bit.

"Still, all was fine. But then in the middle of it, my client stopped speaking, looked around the room and then said, 'You all do more than just Christian music here, right?'"

Hear that pin drop? Yeah, so did everyone else.

"This is Billboard magazine, for cryin' out loud!" Dennis says. "The Bible of the music biz! My first thought was, *'These people think she – and we – are idiots!'* Not exactly the perception you want to make on the trade media, ya know?"

Knowing Dennis, we're pretty sure he turned the event to the artist's advantage and she probably left that meeting smelling like a rose. That's just the kind of magic Dennis knows how to weave. Still, you prefer to save your silver bullets for nightmares that are NOT of your own making. And Dennis is the first to admit the fault did not rest entirely with the artist.

"The mistakes on our end:

"1) I had presumed that my client, a 29-year old graduate of a world-renown college of music, knew that Billboard was THE trade magazine for the music industry, or that she had been briefed by the publicist;

"2) The publicist never thought that this 29-year old artist wouldn't have a better understanding of the magazine since the artist is trying to make a career in commercial music;

"3) And the manager didn't take the lead in making sure his artist was fully prepared.

"The mistake on the artist's part:

"1) She never even thought to ask questions about who the publication was, who they reached, what they wanted to talk about...she simply went to the interview because the publicist, and I, told her to."

Know Thyself

We've already touched on this subject, but it's important enough to come at it from a slightly different perspective. In Shakespeare's tragedy, "Hamlet," Laertes is getting ready to go off to school, and is receiving some sage advice from his father, Polonius. After saying all of the traditional things fathers tell their sons when they are getting ready to fly the nest, Polonius ends with this nugget of wisdom - "Above all, to thine own self be true."

Before you head into your interview, we would say that advice is still true today - *Be true to yourself.* No Bolonius.

Know who you are. Know why you do what you do.

Do you play music for music's sake or is it a ministry? Do you play guitar because it is your job to play guitar and you are good at it?

By the way, doing something because it's your job is okay, even in the Christian market. Most of the writing we do is utilitarian. We do it in order to pay our bills and put food on the table. Mike's goal has always been to write the Great American Novel; and one day, perhaps he will. In the meantime, he doesn't find writing press releases and movie reviews to be a lesser calling.

Years ago, Mike interviewed Sacred Warrior; as heavy a metal band as Christian music had known up to that time. During the conversation, he discovered that not all the band members loved heavy metal music. They played metal because they realized many kids were into metal music and the band used it as a platform to draw people to hear the Gospel. Playing metal music was their job... sort of. All of the band members also worked construction so they could put shoes on their children's feet.

Since we mentioned it earlier, we're assuming that by now you know the niche your particular art form fills. However, in case you're one of *those people* who don't read a book chronologically, let us remind you of the reasons it is important. [Those of you who did read the book beginning with the Prologue can skim through this brief part.]

One of our common questions to musicians is, 'What style of music do you play?' Not that we don't know – we do our homework before an interview - but we want to know what they think about their music. It's not uncommon – especially among new artists – to hear in response, "Oh, I don't want to label my music."

While that may sound cool, it's just not good marketing. If you don't know what style of music you play, how can I find your music in the bin at Wal-Mart? You don't have to nail it down to rap or rock or country. It's okay if you paint your music with a broad stroke, but throw us a bone, here. You can play a range from classical to funk-a-billy, which might sound like a weird combination, but it's intriguing enough for us to want to pursue it in an interview.

Know Thy Audience

Do you like to play in nightclubs or street-corners, trusting the Lord for an opportunity to share the Gospel? Or do you prefer playing at church youth camps? Maybe you would like to play for the Women of Faith© conference or a Promise Keepers© rally. Do you make faith-based films that end with someone getting saved, or do you prefer films that are edgy and gritty yet offer a beam of hope for people who would never darken the door of a church?

Knowing your audience is all a part of defining who you are and what your calling is.

By the way, it's okay if you feel called to minister to the Church. Not everyone is called to be on the frontlines; someone has to keep the home fires burning. It's not like everyone sitting in those pews actually has a relationship with Christ, and even among those who do, life can deal some brutal blows. The Church is as much a hospital for broken folks as it is a cathedral for the saints.

Are you the Great American Novelist, pounding out 120,000 words of heart-pounding adventure to rival Gatsby or Gandalf? Or are you the guy whose 1000 words will challenge "The Pokey Little Puppy" for the title of bestselling children's book of all time?

Are you a standup comedian or Shakespearean actor? Ballet or modern? Fantasy or Non-fiction? It doesn't matter what you do, as long as you *know* what you do and *who* you are doing it for.

Knowing your audience also makes it easier for your team to market you and your stuff. If you know your genre is Christian country, you save your publicist the trouble of contacting "HM Magazine" about doing a feature on you, since they focus on hard music.

Know Thy Medium

We're not talking about the size of your t-shirt. We're

talking about the media format that will publish your interview. We're talking about whether this interview is for print or broadcast; radio or television; magazine or newspaper; blog or podcast; national, regional, or local; religious, secular, or rabidly denominational. Will it be live, or recorded? Will your interviewer be friendly or adversarial?

Interviews play out differently in different mediums. If you are being interviewed for a print publication, the interview might take anywhere from thirty minutes to several hours. It probably won't matter much if you are having problems with hay fever that day, complete with a runny nose and red, itchy eyes, because the person doing the interview will either be taking notes or recording what you have to say. Later, the journalist will transcribe the interview, pull out the good quotes, combine them with background research, and write an article based upon the accumulated information.

If your interview is for a live radio broadcast, or being recorded for a podcast, it probably won't last as long.

"The length of the interview depends upon the format of the station and the content of the interview in relation to the format," Larry Wayne explains. "For radio, I would say that after ten minutes, what needs to be said has been said. In a recorded situation – and I would always vote for recording interviews first so the host can maintain control and focus of the content – your twelve minute interview could be cut to a minute or so."

Knowing this, remember that how you sound will be just as important as what you say. And if you are being interviewed on television, you have the added dimension of how you look and how you dress.

If you are interviewing with the local newspaper about a show you are playing in town, is there a local connect point or tie-in you can use? A local sponsor that you support? A hometown story that the readership can relate to? Does the local event have a tie-in to a national event?

Our friend Holly McClure knows television. She has more than 20 years experience in the entertainment industry as a film critic, talk show host, producer, director, writer and media personality with numerous appearances on FOX, CNN, MSNBC, Politically Incorrect and others. Presently, she is the host of "Holly on Hollywood" and "BTS" [Behind the Scenes] for Parables Network, and serves as the Executive Producer for Parables Network. To get the most out of a television interview, Holly agrees that doing your homework is key.

"Watch the show ahead of time," Holly states. "Observe the host's style. Are they listening to the guest or are they thinking of what they are going to say next? There are some hosts who just love to hear themselves talk and come off as the expert; they will commandeer the interview. You went on the show to discuss your book and you ended up with two minutes of air time while the host spent six minutes of the time talking about another subject."

Most television shows will have a producer call you ahead of time to prepare you. Holly offers a list of question you should ask during this call.

- How long will your interview be? ["If you're going to have 10 minutes, that means that you're probably going to be able to answer about five questions."]

- Will there be breaks during the interview? If so, when will they fall in the interview time?
- Will there be other guests?
- Is it going to be live or taped?
- How they are going to promote your book/CD. Are they going to have your website on the screen? Are they going to hold up a copy of your book? Are they going to put your name and your title on the screen?
- Where should you send a list of questions for the host to ask? Even if the producer says, 'Well, that's okay; our host knows what to ask,' you should find out why they are bringing you on; the topic they're bringing you on for. ["I would be very wary of that," Holly warns. "I would *never* go on an interview and not know what they are going to ask you or how they're going to approach the subject. Sometimes they'll throw you curves. It's important to get as much information ahead of time as you can."]
- What perspective the interview is coming from? If it's a Christian show, great. If it's not, is the host Christian or not; that's imperative to know so that you can gauge your answers accordingly.
- Will they be taking phone calls or not? Some people don't want the surprise of what might come through a phone call. Make it clear to the producer whether you want to take phone calls or not.

Practice. Practice. Practice.

If you are a performing actor, artist, author, singer, songwriter, or stand-up comedian, this word should be familiar to you. Just as you practice your lines for a play or perfect your songs or prepare for a concert, you also need to practice for interviews.

Practice answering questions with your publicist or with a member of your team. Listen for colloquialisms or slang; avoid using 'ah' 'um' or 'ya know' – it comes across amateurish. If you find yourself wandering in the answer, pause and re-do it. Discuss answers that might sound vague or confusing.

When people are nervous, they tend to speak faster. As you practice your answers, slow down and pitch your voice a bit lower, to avoid sounding squeaky or nasal. If you have a recording device, record yourself answering questions; it will give you an idea how you sound over the air. If you don't have a recording device...get one, and record yourself answering questions. Trust us. It will help you.

Practicing may sound silly, it is not. When Paula's book was about to release, the marketing team scheduled several radio interviews. For the first time, she was having to take her own advice on being interviewed. Mike practiced with her several times, asking her questions about the book, the history behind it, the message of it, the goals for it; all the questions an interviewer might ask.

Whereas Paula is quite comfortable interviewing other people, she says *being* interviewed is, "A whole 'nuther critter.'" She found herself stumbling, having brain freezes, getting distracted.

Practicing beforehand brought these problems to the surface where they could be dealt with. She and Mike discussed how to improve her answers and then he asked the question again so she could practice answering...again. And again. Until it no longer sounded rehearsed or stilted.

There is information that you want to convey that you don't

want to leave to chance, so prepare it beforehand. When Paula is interviewed about "YHWH: The Flood, The Fish & The Giant," she always says, "We wrote these stories to take these great characters from the Bible off the flannel board and dress them in flesh and bone."

"Practice until your answers do not feel practiced. Trust me when I say that these practice sessions – and there were a lot of practice sessions – helped tremendously," says Paula. "It made me more comfortable when the real interviews came along. It also comes in handy if your interviewer is less than fully prepared, which will happen."

Taboo Areas

Just as it is important to know areas you want to cover during an interview, it is also important to know those areas you are *not* willing to discuss. These areas – and the reasons they are sensitive - are unique to each person, so we are not going to list them here.

Some artists will let the interviewer know ahead of time – either through the confirmation email or through their publicist – the areas they don't wish to discuss. Mike has had the opportunity to interview Academy Award winner, Jon Voight, on more than one occasion. The last time was a telephone interview. Beforehand, Mr. Voight's publicist requested that Mike not ask questions about Mr. Voight's relationship with his daughter, Angelina Jolie. Mike, of course, honored that request.

Does that mean those questions will not come up during the interview? Not at all. There are some journalists who go after those topics like sharks to blood. [Whoops! Did we just call them sharks? Well, if the fishy shoe fits...]

So, how do you handle them? Go back and read Holly McClure's suggestions again. They are valuable for not only television, but all interview situations.

You may get a trap question. Laugh and politely say, "You know, I'm not here to discuss my personal life today; our concert to raise money for the homeless shelter is the more important topic." Or "The more important issue here is Habitat for Humanity" [or whatever is the reason you're being interviewed]. If the host comes back and asks, "But, are you *insert whatever trap question applies to you?*" just laugh and say, "Really? No; I'm not going to go there." Then smile and say nothing. Leave the ball in their court.

Smile. That's another key factor. Make eye contact, be confident, smile, be energetic and sparkling – think *Jazz Hands!* ...except with your eyes.

Holly McClure speaks about trap questions from personal experience. She had been invited to be a guest on Bill Maher's TV show, "Politically Incorrect," twenty-one times. The producer explained Holly's attitude during interviews as one of the main reasons for her repeat invitations.

"The producer told me, 'Even when Bill Maher is pressuring you, you smile and always have a confidence and you're always pleasant. That's one of the reasons we have you on the show; you resonate with the viewers and you're still pleasant,'" Holly recalls.

"During one time on the show, Bill Maher said, 'What if I don't believe in your #@$ Jesus or your ^%&$ God?' The audience gasped. I smiled and said, 'Well, you don't have to accept it. That's the beauty about being a Christian, Bill; you have a choice. You have free will.' When we walked off the show, he patted my back and said, 'Great job, Holly!'"

From then on, Holly realized that even when you're discussing a controversial topic and people are trying to badger you, if you just smile and remain pleasant, you gain the sympathy of the viewer.

Dress to Impress

Just as the right clothes are important for a head shot, wearing the right clothes also is important for an interview. There are no hard and fast rules that apply to all interview situations, but there are some guidelines.

Dress for your audience. What you would wear to an interview with a journalist for the Rolling Stone may be different from what you would wear to an interview with ParentLife.

Dress for the media. You might not think that your wardrobe matters much for an interview for a print publication, but what if the interviewer brings along a photographer? Surely you wardrobe doesn't matter during a radio interview - unless you are wearing clunky jewelry that keeps banging against the microphone. Avoid wearing jewelry that makes noise or remove it before the interview begins. For television, avoid busy or wild patterns that play havoc with the camera, and don't wear white, green, or red shirts. White washes you out and green makes you disappear in front of a green screen and red make you look flushed. As an extra precaution, take several outfits and ask the director which works best.

Ladies, keep your makeup neutral and light. For television, check with the person who scheduled the interview to see if they are going to put makeup on you. If so, find out how early you need to arrive.

No matter what you wear, good hygiene is of utmost importance.
- Don't eat spicy foods before the interview.
- Use breath mints that don't color your tongue.
- Don't wear perfume or cologne. Some people have severe allergies to them.

Pre-Interview Odds and Ends

Who's talking? If you're a band, or a group from a show's cast, determine who will talk about what topics during the interview. It is important, however, for everyone to be able to discuss all topics in the event that the flu ravages your band and you are the only one well enough to be interviewed.

Find out how the interviewer conducts their interviews. Whereas Mike and Paula record their interviews, some journalists sit with a notebook computer on their lap and type out everything, never once making eye contact with the interviewee.

If you're going to an interview with a journalist you have never met before, it's a good idea to find out what the journalist looks like. Go to their website and print up a copy of their picture. Imagine how embarrassing it can be to be sitting in a restaurant, wondering why the person you're meeting with is so late. You finally call their cell phone, only to discover they were sitting across the room from you, wondering why you were so late. It happens. Trust us.

The day before the interview, confirm all the details of the interview, including time and location.

Restaurant chains may have more than one location in a town. You don't want to show up at the wrong place. If you have never been to the location before, get directions, or better yet, take a practice drive out there, in order to confirm the location and how long it takes to arrive.

Check the weather. Heavy rains or snow/ice will significantly slow down traffic. Don't forget to take into account the time of day you're driving; what might normally take 30 minutes to drive will be different during rush hour traffic or if you have to drive past a school zone when children are being dropped off or picked up.

Confirm all pertinent phone numbers. For phone interviews, confirm who is calling whom and what number will be used. Try to get a back up phone number in case your service goes out unexpectedly.

Stuff to Take

When it comes to prepping for an interview, Murphy's Law is in full effect. If you are running late, chances are you will forget to take your press kit. Or you will spill your coffee in your lap. Or the Internet will go out.

You can outwit Murphy, but it takes proper prior planning. Gather the stuff you need for the interview the night before. Put it in a convenient place where you don't have to search for it. Have a backup plan. And always, always have the contact information of the person you are supposed to meet or talk to, so you can let her know if you are going to be delayed or need to reschedule.

It never hurts to keep *a just in case* bag in the trunk of your car, for those moments when Murphy shows up. The bag might contain:

- A change of clothes - *just in case* you spill your coffee on your shirt while you're driving to the radio station.
- Breath mints - *just in case* you drank your coffee and have raging coffee breath.
- Hair and makeup stuff - *just in case* you need a touch up.
- Blotting tissues - *just in case* your face gets shiny.
- Toothbrush and toothpaste - *just in case* you discover that pepper corn in your teeth.
- Extra press kit and a copy of your book, CD, DVD, etc - *just in case* your publicist failed to send one to the interviewer.
- Extra cell phone battery - *just in case* your cell phone dies.
- The intervener's cell phone number - *just in case* you, or she, is running late.
- Money - *just in case* you need to pick up the tab for coffee or a meal.
- Notes - *just in case* you need to quote important information or statistics.

The Interview

The big day has arrived. You are set for your interview. But there are a couple of last minute items you really should attend to be for shaking hands with the interviewer, or answering that phone call:

- Go to the bathroom. Nerves can play havoc on your bladder.

- While you are in the bathroom, check yourself out in the mirror - hair, teeth, makeup.
- Pop a breath mint into your mouth. Just be sure to finish it before you start the interview. There is nothing worse than your interviewer having to perform the Heimlich Maneuver on you because you start choking on a breath mint in the middle of your interview.
- Grab a bottle of water. You will get a tickle in your throat, or your mouth will go dry, or you will just need to have an excuse to pause before answering a question.
- Say a prayer for peace, calm, a clear mind, and gracious speech.
- Mute your cell phone and put it away. Better yet, turn your cell phone off. [If your wife is about to go into labor, you can leave your cell phone on - just let your interviewer know that you might get an emergency call. Yes, it has happened to us during an interview.]
- Place your notes where they are handy but don't fiddle with them.

Meeting the Interviewer

Find ways to connect to the person you are interviewing with. Mention something you learned about them during your pre-interview research. You can find out a lot about a person simply by being observant. How do they dress – formal or casual? How do they speak – eloquent, educated, rustic, hip? Are they comfortable and at ease, or nervous and tongue-tied?

Is your interviewer wearing an unusual piece of jewelry? Is there some significance to it, i.e. a wedding ring, family crest, a class ring, a religious symbol? If the interview is at the interviewer's office, check out the décor, the pictures on the wall, the books on the shelf, memorabilia. Is there something there that sparks a connect point?

Is there a picture of their child or grandchild? A compliment on a child goes a long way toward winning a friend.

Phone Interviews

One of the blessings of phone interviews is that they can be done from the comfort of your home. One of the challenges of phone interviews is that they can be done from the comfort of your home.

Give yourself some time to prepare for your phone interview. A half an hour before the call time is generally sufficient, but you know what you need.

Go to the bathroom, get a glass of water, and gather your notes. Children and pets need to be in another part of the house. Paula and Mike, as well as Torry, have multiple dogs that can be quite noisy. During interviews, they either go outside or in another part of the house. Recording equipment can pick up a dog barking on the other side of your door. If you gave the interviewer a secondary number to call, have the other phone handy. You can't predict when your phone company might decide to work on their tower, temporarily cutting out service.

If more than one person, such as you and two of your band mates, are doing a phone interview, make sure you each identify yourselves when you speak. You may know who you are, but the interviewer probably won't - particularly if they don't get around to transcribing the interview for a week.

In Person Interviews

While Mike and Paula have interviewed people in locations as varied as a corporate board room, an artist's basement studio, or sitting on the floor in a back hall of a hotel during Gospel Music Week, most of their in person interviews take place in public locations such as restaurants.

Public locations have the challenge of being... well... public. Another one of Murphy's laws is that when you conduct an interview in a public place you will always run into old friend. And even if you don't, chances are the interviewer will.

"While we would never want someone we are interviewing to be rude to an old acquaintance, time really is money - for us and for the person we are interviewing," Mike explains. "We may only have 30 minutes scheduled for the interview. We don't have time to wait while they get caught up on old times. A fellow journalist told us the story of interviewing a rising young artist during GMA week. Another well-known recording star walked by and the artist jumped up to talk with him. 15 minutes later, she came back to resume the interview...just as our journalist friend was packing up her recorder to head off to her next interview. Did she write a story about the artist? What do you think?"

If you encounter a friend or acquaintance during an interview, be polite, greet them, introduce them to the interviewer and promise to call them later. Then get back to the interview.

Be prepared to pick up the tab for the coffee. Some journalists are on an expense account and may cover the cost, but many journalists are not. You can avoid awkward moments by being prepared to pay.

Good manners are always appropriate, but during an in person interview they are a must. We're not talking about lifting your pinky finger while holding a coffee cup (which, by the way, is really more about balance than style). We're talking about basic table manners, such as napkin in your lap, elbows off the table, and not talking while you're chewing your food. Proper table manners have never hurt anyone, but poor table manners leave a terrible impression. If your parents didn't teach you good manners, check out a book or look them up online and learn them. There are no excuses.

If you're in a public place and the interviewer is recording your conversation, there are likely to be numerous other conversations going on around you. Slow down and speak clearly. You don't want the interviewer to have to try to guess what you said.

Radio Interviews

Radio interviews have their own unique challenges. Doug Griffin, the "Doug" half of the Salem Music Network's "Family Friendly Morning Show with Doug and Jaci," is a master of the radio interview. He has some incredibly important advice about what NOT to do.

"Don't cuss or slap the host," Doug jokingly admonishes. As Christians, avoiding 'cussing' should be a no-brainer, but there are plenty of words that don't exactly fall into the category of 'cussing' but may not be appropriate for use on

Christian radio. When it doubt, just don't use them.

On a more positive note, Doug suggests that you try to find out the goals of the station and then make them work with what you want to accomplish.

"Some good questions to ask before you go on the air are: Is this a long form/talk format, like news or talk radio, or is this a music format, like our show? In the latter case, be brief, but direct. Have a few things down solid that you want to say.

"Don't feel like you are talking to *everyone out there in Radioland*," Doug advises. "Just talk as if you were talking to one person. If you are working with a broadcast team, such as myself and Jaci, don't just talk to the one host. Talk to both of us."

Larry Wayne agrees. "Consider the interview as a conversation between two friends. You might want to send the host a few suggested questions, but some hosts may want to wander from any kind of suggested questions, so be prepared to not know exactly what is coming. Consider it an opportunity to show off your personality!"

It's alright to have some notes handy during a radio interview to make sure you get your facts straight, particularly if you are doing a phoner. There's nothing worse than telling your audience that you are going to be in concert tonight at 7p.m. at 12th and Porter, when in fact you are playing at the Ace of Clubs at 9p.m.; or to forget to mention to the listeners where they can get copies of your new book.

Monosyllabic answers make for horrible interviews,

according to Doug. He also warns against not being prepared, copping an attitude, and not being awake.

"It's tough if you overslept, missed the bus, etc.," Doug declares. "But you've got this limited amount of time with your radio audience. You should make the most of it."

Be enthusiastic. Radio is a high energy medium and it works best when you are passionate about your subject. Believe it or not, people can _hear_ you smile. Think we're joking? Next time you have a telemarketer on the phone, listen to their spiel. Can you tell if they are reading a canned script? Can you tell if they are enthusiastic? Can you imagine their face on the other end of the line? Can you tell if they smiling? Sure you can. Folks on the other side of the radio can tell, too.

Avoid making excess noise. During an interview with Doug Griffin for her book, Paula tried to reiterate a point by tapping on the desk. "Out of the corner of my eye, I saw Mike, who was standing in the corner watching, straighten up and make a small _Stop it_ gesture. I suddenly realized what I had been doing, and stopped."

Doug says the best interviews happen with people who are not afraid to be real, who are not afraid to let their guard down. "You need to have that 'fire' in you - even at 6 AM," he insists. "Great radio is having someone tell you a great story. You should hear how Tammy Trent tells her story about losing her husband - about their love - the loss - the recovery. That kind of interview is awesome!"

Unless you are on NPR, this is not the time to go off on a dissertation. Remember, this is the Attention-Deficit, Jump/Cut, MTV generation. When you think of radio, think in sound bites. According to Larry Wayne, a sound bite is, *"the only :15 seconds the station may use out of that ten minute interview you did."* There is a reason the average pop song only lasts three and a half minutes. Just answer the question. Say what you have to say. Then be quiet and let the other guy talk.

Many radio interviews are recorded. One advantage to this is that if you make a mistake, you can start over and the DJ will clean it up later before airing the interview. It's not wise to rely on this to occur, as Paula learned.

"I was scheduled to be interviewed by a Canadian radio station and, according to the confirmation email from my marketing team, it was going to be recorded for airing later," Paula recalls.

"I called the station and chatted with the DJ for a moment. Then he said, 'I've got to do the news and then we'll do the interview.'

"I felt my heart jump. 'This is going to be *live?*' I asked.

"'We're having problems with our recording equipment,' the DJ said. 'I hope a live interview is alright with you?'

"What was I going to say? 'No?' Of course not. Even though my heart was pounding, I told him it was fine. As I waited for the news to finish, I reminded myself to speak slowly, remember the important facts, avoid 'ums' and dead air, and sound enthusiastic. It turned out to be a great interview, but it could have been a disaster!"

Television Interviews

You're going to be interviewed on television. While that is a big opportunity for you, there are challenges that are unique to interviews in this media.

At some point in our lives, we've all heard, "Sit up straight." Good posture does not mean ram-rod stiff; it means sitting up, holding your shoulders back and your tummy in. Good posture is important in life. It is imperative on television. Good Posture:
- makes you appear excited and interesting.
- allows you to breathe deeply, which helps you relax.
- makes you 'appear' slimmer. Remember, TV really does add 10 pounds.

Our eyes tend to follow motion. During a television interview, you want the audience's attention on what you are saying, not what you are doing. Keep your body still, but not stiff. Don't jiggle your ankles or knees to relieve nervousness. Ladies, cross your legs at the ankles only. Guys, if you wear a tie, please don't play with it.

Gesturing is okay, but keep it to a minimum and keep it controlled. A colleague shared that while relating a crazy incident, she waved her hands wildly and inadvertently smacked the host's face, giving her a bloody nose *while on air.*

Advice for All Interviews

Although it has been mentioned before, it is important enough for us to say it again. To re-state; speak clearly, slowly and distinctly. Avoid colloquialisms and slang. Mike's mother has a favorite saying, "You ain't just a bird chirping." Now some people might know that quaint phrase means, "You're correct," but not everyone would.

Pay attention. Really listen to the questions. It will keep you from talking over your host. While nature hates a vacuum and nobody likes dead air, it is perfectly acceptable to take a pregnant pause to consider an answer to a question.

Even worse than dead air is the ubiquitous, "Um," Uh," "You know," and "Like." Learn to speak without these killer-fillers. This is not as easy as it sounds. Just try talking on any given subject for thirty seconds straight without resorting to one of those place holders and you'll see what we mean.

Use concrete - not abstract – language, and keep it simple. Remember, you are trying to appeal to a broad, cross-section of readers or listeners. Don't worry about trying to sound hip and cool. Just be honest and be yourself. The Truth is hip and cool enough.

There are two deadly answers to an interviewer's questions: "Yes," and "No." Avoid them like the plague. Sometimes you will get an inexperienced interviewer who will ask a 'yes or no' question. Try to answer with an explanation rather than just an affirmative.

Remember, "Yes, because…" or "No, because…"

Think in sound bites and great quotes. This makes the interviewer's job easier and they'll thank you for it.

Keep in mind the old adage, 'Why buy the cow when you can get the milk for free?' Tempt your audience with just enough information that makes them want to learn more.

The idea is to get them to buy your book or CD, to encourage them to go see your new movie, or come to the concert. Always leave 'em wanting more. And don't feel that, simply because the microphone is in still in front of you that you have to keep talking.

"Be gracious, patient and helpful in the interview process," Melissa Campbell Goodson encourages her artists. "Your interviewer could be extremely nervous or unprepared or inexperienced. Know that every publication and radio station is entirely different and that the interview experience and conversational style totally varies from person to person."

Be positive. Smile.

Time Wasters

Don't waste the interviewer's time. One year during Gospel Music Week, Mike and Paula interviewed a new band that was made up of a group of kids who were not too far removed from their high school years.

"We could tell from their behavior that they didn't take these interviews seriously," Paula recalls. "They thought it would be great fun to play a trick on us by changing their names when they answered our questions. Did we write an article about them? No, we did not. Do we remember who they were? Yes, we do. Will we ever interview them again? You be the judge."

When You Assume...

If you don't know the interviewer personally, don't assume he is your friend, or that she shares your views.

A colleague related this story of a Christian author who was being interviewed on a live, secular radio program. Everything was going nicely until they went to commercial break. At that point, the host turned to the author and began railing against conservative Christianity, calling many prominent leaders hypocrites and generally filling the air with vile, intense hatred for the entire two-minute break. Once they were back on the air the host immediately pasted a beatific smile on his face and announced, 'And now back to our guest.'

As you can imagine, the author was thrown completely off her guard by the diatribe during the break. She stumbled over her words and appeared - at least in her own mind - completely incoherent, a perfect example of the host's version of an ignorant, conservative Christian who couldn't put two intelligent sentences together.

The host had accomplished his mission. His stealth approach to sabotaging his guest worked flawlessly by putting her off center just long enough, and then putting her on a live microphone.

The lesson to be learned: always be on your guard and remain focused no matter what sort of distractions may be thrown your way.

Conversely, you may find allies in unlikely places. Who would think Lilith Fair would be the launching pad for Sixpence None the Richer? Or that influential Dallas radio DJ, Big Gay Jim, would be a huge fan of MercyMe's "I Can Only Imagine?"

As the Master said, "Be as wise as serpents, and as harmless as doves."

Is that your final answer?

Mike explains that he and Paula almost always end their interviews with this simple statement: "I hate leaving an interview without giving you the last word, because I'm afraid you've got a really great answer to a question I neglected to ask. Is there something that you wanted to talk about that we didn't?"

Most interviewers worth their salt will have a similar last question.

Why?

Because we know that once you think the interview is over, you relax and talk about things that are really important. We let the tape roll and let you talk. Some of our best feature articles have come from this simple, little question.

Yet many people we have interviewed say, 'No, I think you've covered everything.'

This is a hint: ALWAYS, ALWAYS, **ALWAYS** have a last word.

If there truly is something that you wanted to talk about, but we chased a bunny trail and didn't get to it, this is your chance. Even if we did cover everything you wanted to say, this is your opportunity to hammer home that one most important point that you wanted to make.

I have a new CD coming out. It will be available Tuesday exclusively at Family Christian Stores.
My new novel just came out. You can get it at Amazon.com.
We're in concert tonight at First Baptist Church.

Go see my new movie!

If you are given the opportunity to have the last word, use it.

The End

End the interview by politely shaking the interviewer's hand and thanking them. They have hundreds of people who would love to be interviewed and they chose to interview you. You should be grateful.

After the interview, ask the journalist if you can have a copy of the article, link to the article, or an mp3 or video of the interview. Don't bother asking to see an advance copy of an article. Few magazines will agree to this, beyond providing you with direct quotes that you can check for accuracy.

While it is never a good idea to believe your own press [at least not too much], you should at least read it from time to time. It is a good idea to see how you are perceived in print. This will help you shape the way you participate in future interviews.

One Mile Rule

Remember our 'last word' advice? Well, there is a slight variation to that rule and to illustrate it, we use a story about former President Jimmy Carter.

In 1976, when Mr. Carter was still Governor of Georgia and running for President, he was interviewed for an article in Playboy magazine [probably not the best choice of publications to accept an interview from, but we digress]. After the interview was 'over,' on his way out the reporter asked off-handedly whether the governor had ever lusted after a woman who was not his wife. "Yes," Mr. Carter replied, "I have lusted in my heart."

Guess what the headline for that article was?

The moral of this story is; the interview is never over until you are a mile away. By the way, this also applies to any time you are dealing with the public. If you had a really bad experience at a concert venue, you are better off not discussing it with the rest of your band until you are a mile down the road. You never know who is listening.

Interview Faux Pas

"Never say anything negative about the town in which you are being interviewed," Dennis Disney says.

He recalls one of his clients doing a radio interview in Nashville while she was considering moving to Nashville from Seattle. The radio interviewer asked her how she liked Nashville, and she said...on-air... 'I don't like Nashville as much as I like Seattle.'

"In the first place, that wasn't the question," Dennis exclaims. "The question was, 'How do you like Nashville?'

"Second, she could've answered that question in so many more diplomatic ways: *'I'm just learning Nashville, but I really like the people and the culture, etc.'* She could always add something like, *'Nashville is so new to me right now that my heart is still in Seattle, but so far the people in town have really welcomed me and made feel at home.'* She could've said anything other than, 'I don't like Nashville as much as I like Seattle!' Not the best way to win friends in the city you're trying to win over, ya know?"

A variation of this faux pas is when you make negative comments about interviewers in public; you never know whether their mother or BFF is sitting at the table next to you.

Good Advice

As you conduct more and more interviews, chances are you are going to hear the same questions over and over. That's because everyone wants to know the same thing, and chances are the guy asking the questions in Peoria didn't hear your interview last night in Dallas. You will be tempted to get bored or frustrated with it.

Don't.

Just because you've heard yourself give the same answer a dozen times doesn't mean the local audience has. The number two rule in theatre, right after, *The Show Must Go On*, is: *The audience on the last night of the play paid just as much as the audience on opening night, and they deserve the same, enthusiastic performance. It is your obligation to deliver it.*

So, deliver it.

Debrief

Once the interview is over, it's time to debrief and evaluate it with your Team. What did you do right? What did you do wrong? Were there questions that you did not expect? How did you handle them? How could you handle them better next time?

[Un]common Courtesy

A handwritten thank you note goes a long, long way. Early in his writing career, Mike was invited to interview Sparrow Records hot, new modern rock band, The Waiting.

"I met the band at Sparrow's corporate office in Brentwood, Tennessee. We hit it off immediately and had a great conversation," Mike says. "I pitched the idea to "Christian Single Magazine" and ended up writing a feature article about the band and I also reviewed their new album for that magazine.

"Before they knew where - or even if - the article would be published, I received a very nice thank you note in the mail, signed by each member of the band.

"I was completely taken aback. Although I had written numerous reviews and feature articles about artists in the Christian music industry, I had never received a thank you note from anyone I had interviewed.

"Please understand; I love The Waiting. I loved The Waiting when they were on the now defunct R.E.X. label, and I loved what they did on Sparrow and later on InPop. I still think Brad Olsen is one of the most brilliant and gifted songwriters of our age. But that little, polite thank you note made me a fan for life. And it compelled me to pitch them whenever and wherever I could."

In the years that followed, Mike and Paula have interviewed thousands of people and have received less than a handful of thank you notes. They have kept every one of them.

"Each one of those notes have made an impact on us," Paula

insists.

We make it a practice to send out a handwritten thank you note whenever one of us is interviewed. Besides being a great marketing tool, it's just [un]common courtesy.

Handling Publicity

Interviews, feature articles and reviews are great publicity tools. Scan a copy of the article and save it to your computer's hard drive. Make a back up copy and store it on line or on a disk. Computers crash. You don't want to lose your information.

If the article is online - and it's positive - leave a comment, thanking them for the great article, kind comments, understanding what you are trying to accomplish - whatever fits the article. Link the article to your website and then include a link from FaceBook, MySpace, Twitter or whatever social media site you use.

Chapter Five

Branding

By now you probably feel like a self-promoting expert and we wish you all the best with your own shameless self-promotion. We have and continue to promote ourselves, including the projects we work on that are not indie. However, we also realize the need to continue learning more about promotion, in order to hopefully make our next project easier.

Throughout this book, we've encouraged you to seek expert advice and aid when and where you can. With this in mind we would like to introduce you to our friend, marketing expert Kevin Tucker.

Kevin Tucker is the founder/creative director – although he prefers to be called the *Director of Momentum* - of Collide: A Creative Studio, a boutique design and creative consulting company in the Nashville, Tennessee area. Kevin's wife Becky works alongside him as the *Director of Trajectory*.

We wanted to include Kevin's thoughts on marketing, specifically concerning 'branding.' Much of the following information comes from Kevin's knowledge and experience. Some of Kevin's advice may apply to where you are now in your shameless self-promotion journey, while some of it may be gleaned, winnowed and stored away for future projects.

Meet Kevin Tucker
Kevin has over fourteen years of experience creating powerful visual communications, working with a variety of clients in diverse industries. He oversees an array of freelance talent and seasonal design interns to create print, web/interactive, and brand identity work for a variety of clients and projects in the entertainment, publishing, consumer products, healthcare, Christian ministry, and tourism industries, among other small businesses and organizations.

The goal of Collide Creative falls under the philosophy of bringing "The Moment Of Impact" to the intended audience through effective, strategic use of design, and bringing a sense of personality and character that is unique to each brand.

When asked who he has worked with, Kevin – a humble man – directs people to his website. Past clients and projects that Kevin and Collide Creative have worked with include Larry the Cable Guy, Amy Grant, Big & Rich, Sandi Patty, Bill Engvall, Phil Keaggy, Mark Schultz, Jaci Velasquez, Pepsi, Warner Bros. Records, Sony Music Nashville, EMI Christian Music, Word Entertainment, The

Village Chapel, Healthspring, Austin Peay State University, Shoney's, Prevent Child Abuse Tennessee, Billy Graham Evangelical Association, FiveStone Studios, Cabedge, VF Imagewear and Dye VanMol & Lawrence.

Branding [as in Marketing... not Cattle]

When you talk business with Kevin, you'll often hear him refer to 'branding.' For those who do not have a clear idea of what that is, Kevin explains.

"A brand is a reputation, an impression that people have of a product or service. Outside of making a quality product, the process of *branding* includes photos, an image, a cover, a symbol, a logo; all of these are components of the brand.

"The first component of a brand is having something that is valuable, something that people would want, that they tell their friends about. If you don't have something that is worth branding, then no amount of PR is going to make people want it.

"The whole process of branding is a systematic effort; to get that first impression and make that first impression last; to communicate to people what you want them to know and what you want them to remember about your product or service."

Sometimes branding can work too well. *Kleenex,* for instance, is a brand of facial tissues, but people commonly use the name as a generic term to refer to any and all tissues.

When designing the different components of a brand, you want to make an impact that is meaningful – why is your product/services the best – and not just lasting.

Symbols

Most people would easily recognize the company logos for Coca-Cola, Apple, MacDonald's or the image of Uncle Sam representing the United States. These are powerful symbols that resonate with the entire population.

"When people see these images, they know what they mean," Kevin states. "They get it, they feel it, they have a response to it. People remember these symbols, which is very important. You may love these companies or products - or you may hate them - but you know their symbols.

"There is so much reputation wrapped up in that symbol. The symbol doesn't *say* that; it just reminds you of that reputation. So whatever image you're talking about - a website, an album cover – you recognize it and have a response. If it is new, then the first time you see it, that symbol is forming an impression.

"A logo is the simplest form of saying everything about your brand and because it's a simple image, many people think it's a simple process. But from one who has done a lot of logos, it is one of the most difficult things for a designer to create. You're trying to distill so much meaning down to a simple image. If a logo is too complex, people are going to ignore it and if it's too generic, it's not going to stand out."

Slogans or Tag Lines

Brands also include slogans or tag lines. You might not remember the crown over the name, but if someone says, *"When you care enough to send the very best,"* chances are you'll think of Hallmark.

"People know that meaning," Kevin says. "They get teary-eyed over the moving commercials. You get the impression that Hallmark is an important way of expressing an emotion. Then there is the Hallmark Channel and you know what to expect when you watch it - programming that is wholesome and will tug at your heartstrings.

"That slogan says so many things in a simple form; it puts them at a higher level of quality. *They're the very best*...but...*you have to care enough.* Conversely, if you send another brand card, you obviously *don't* care enough. It establishes in peoples' minds the *quality* of what you're offering and Hallmark really did that with their slogan. I don't know why they are the best cards, except that they say so; and they say so convincingly. It has been ingrained into our social psyche that Hallmark cards are the best."

Branding Myself - When Do I Start?

Why, at the very beginning, of course.

"You need to think about what's involved in branding when you're forming the ideas of your project," Kevin explains. "This prevents the process from being rushed just to get the physical product or the website out there."

First Things First

Before rushing to the drawing board or firing up your computer to begin branding yourself, there is an important thing to take into consideration.

"Branding depends upon who you are or what your product

or service is," Kevin states. "It must also take into account who you are going to pursue with your marketing. My first question to anybody, when they are seeking to initiate a branding process, '*Who* are you speaking to and *what* kind of message do you want them to hear?' This has to be determined before you even start talking about *how* you get that message out there."

Your audience is either consumer-focused – where you want them to buy a product; or industry-focused – where you want them to buy a service. That focus may vary from situation to situation. An actor might be promoting himself to directors and casting agents, but at the same time he is promoting the film he wants people to see.

What Do You Want?

Another preliminary step is to define what you want people to respond to and what you want them to do.

"You want to motivate the people to some kind of action," Kevin states. "You want them to buy your product, go to your concert, to find someone to book you, to cast you. If you don't do this, things gets muddy."

While this might seem obvious, people make this mistake all the time with their marketing materials. A comedian or musician's website may have all kinds of information and images, but unless there is a call to action, it leaves people wondering, *What do you want me to do?*

"Every ad has to have a call to action; otherwise you're wasting your money," Kevin explains. "What do you want people to do? You want them to buy something, right? It seems obvious, but it is your responsibility to make it clear to them what you want them to do."

While this is as much about advertising as it is branding, it is important to keep in mind that everything you're driving people towards needs to be about what you want them to do.

Christian Media Brands

When it comes to Christian media branding, Kevin suggests dividing your efforts into the three main sub-categories:

1. Family-friendly entertainment that is not offensive to an audience, yet it is not Christian-specific. Think of films like "Pollyanna," or books like, "Where the Red Fern Grows."
2. Another category is the church audience product; something that you can promote through a church, such as youth ministry videos, or sermon notes based on a popular feature film.
3. The last category is evangelical message that is intended to go out to the general public. This is where films like, "Facing the Giants" fit.

Whatever category your project fits into, remember that you are not just competing with things on a Christian bookstore shelf. You're also competing with everything people are exposed to in the mainstream as well. Make your comparisons of who your audiences are in both worlds.

Challenges for Christian Brands

Christian media has unique challenges, because there are limitations as far as content and imaging. You have to be in the safe zone, image-wise; you don't want to compromise your message by distracting somebody with something they are uncomfortable with. Yet, even this is hard, because there are a lot of people who are uncomfortable with a lot of things.

You're always going to have the fringe crazies who are going to write and say something like - _The type placement on this album caused me to stumble, because it pointed towards the lady's bosom._ While you can't please all of the people all of the time, you don't want something that is obviously provocative.

The primary image should tell the audience what is great about the project. A lot of times the message gets muddled up by having a pretty picture of the actor or singer. The mainstream media does it all the time. After all, in the mainstream, it's all about you.

While you do want your audience to remember that _you are_ the singer/songwriter, in Christian media it is _not_ all about you. It has to be more meaningful - there is more message, more concept – than a lot of other media; and this can be a challenge. Making things too glamour and fashion oriented, especially where performing artists are involved, may not necessarily be appropriate, but the alternative may be to use really cliché imagery, which is a bad mistake, too. The last thing you want people to do is roll their eyes at it. You want to come across as culturally relevant or people are not going to take you seriously. It's a fine line.

Kevin admits that competing with mainstream brands is a challenge for all Christian creatives. Mainstream artists tend to have more money and resources at their disposal. His advice to Christian artists - 'Keep on keeping on.'

"Put your best foot forward and use the resources you have to your best ability."

Resources for Branding Elements

Throughout this book, we have told you to begin with your network when looking for a photographer, bio writer or other promotional needs. When you are ready to hire a professional, Kevin says that is still the best advice. Turn to your network first for recommendations.

"Reputation depends upon word of mouth," he explains. "If your network doesn't know anyone, look on the liner notes of a CD cover you like; it usually lists the designer's name."

You can check professional organizations for a list of their members. If you're looking for a photographer, check out the American Society for Media Photographers. To find a designer, check out AIGA.

"This not to say that every good photographer or designer is a member of that organization," Kevin admits, "but it might at least be a starting point."

Even if you think you cannot afford their services, set up a meeting with these people. "Most of these people will sit down with you for half an hour and discuss your needs. It can't hurt to buy a cup of coffee for someone who might be one of your greatest allies in getting your message out."

Choosing a Professional

So, you've got a list of professional photographers, graphic designers or web designers. You've checked out their website and are appropriately impressed with their work.

How do you know which one to choose?

An obvious plus is their personality. After all, you will be working with them; if you don't get along with them, chances are you will not like the results. This is especially true for photographers.

"It's important for a photographer to be personable, to be friendly," Kevin insists. "No matter how good they are with a camera, if they're intimidating when you're standing in front of them then your photos are not going to be any good."

Cutting Costs

Okay, let's just say it; it costs money to hire professionals. Sadly, while the old saying, "You get what you pay for," doesn't hold true in every case; it's true in enough in most cases - particularly in this day and age when anyone with Adobe Photoshop thinks he is a graphic designer.

And it's not just independent artists who are concerned with money. Even established artists have to recover production costs before they earn a profit.

Can you cut costs when hiring a professional? Yes!

"Maybe you can do a half-day photo shoot instead of a full day," Kevin suggests. "Maybe you don't need a full-blown website. Maybe you just need a page that has an image and a button that sends customers to Amazon where they can order your product, or to your actor's reel on YouTube. You can always start with the basics and add more content later as you need it."

When you're building a website, remember what it is you want people to do.

"We (Collide) did Torry Martin's website," Kevin says, "and when we were talking with him, we realized that the main purpose for his website is to get bookings for his comedy. His website does a lot of things under a lot of different sections, but the main purpose was to get bookings. We centered the website around accomplishing that.

"The main thing you see is a big shiny button that says *"Book Torry Now for Your Church, Social Community Group or Business."* You dig around on his site, and you'll find a lot more stuff; his writing, his acting – you can see his actor's reel – but the main thing is the main thing."

Chapter Six

The Power of Networking

Schmoozing, working the room, old boys' club, you scratch my back and I'll scratch yours...whatever you call it, networking often gets a bad rap - and sometimes deservedly so. When networking is used solely for your own gain, it is selfish. And shameful.

However, as we mentioned in the Prologue [you *have* read the Prologue by now, haven't you?] Torry Martin is a master at networking from a different perspective. His unique approach to networking eschews the common idea of *'what can you do for me,'* and turns it around with a *'how can I help you?'* attitude that is both godly and powerful. It's what we call shameless self promotion, because there is nothing shameful about it.

Why Network?

"It's not what you know, it's who you know."

Truer words have not been spoke by man nor beast, especially in the entertainment industry. Even though what you know is vitally important - you do, after all, have to be able to deliver the goods once you get your shot at the big time - you will rarely get your shot at the big time unless somebody gives you that shot. Chances are that _somebody_ is a person you met through networking.

But networking is not, or at least should not be, a one way street. It is not about chatting up perfect strangers in order to find a new business contact. It's not about using your friends to get a leg up in the industry. It is a two-way exchange that benefits all parties involved. Networking puts you in contact with people who can benefit from what you do to you, but it is also about you introducing others to people who can benefit from what they do.

Networking is all about living in community, even if that community is stretched out across the city or across the country. The more well connected to your community you are, the more in-demand you're likely to be.

The advantages to networking are legion. Networking helps you:
- Meet key players in your industry
- Develop professional relationships within your industry
- Keep current on trends in your industry
- Expands your support base of like-minded professionals
- Exchange resources

- Enhances your creative energy
- Create new opportunities
- Build friendships

The Art of Networking

Networking doesn't happen by itself, and it doesn't happen in a vacuum. If you are going to build a successful network you are going to have to work at it, regularly and systematically. You have to treat it as another part of your business routine. But networking is at least as much an art form as it is a science, and sometimes finesse is required to make it work.

Like any other business objective, you need a goal for your networking efforts. This should not be some amorphous, nebulous something. Your networking goals should be concrete, measurable and definable. Write them down. If you can't write them down, they are not clear enough.

Your goal might be to spend :30 minutes each day promoting a friend or colleague to someone who needs their services. Your goal might be to attend one media event each week and meet one new person. Whatever your networking goal is, it must coincide with what you want to accomplish in your career or ministry.

Before you begin networking, you need to determine what you hope to achieve through your efforts. Boil it down to a elevator pitch. In other words, you need to be able to state your goal to another person in the time it would take to ride in an elevator. You must have a specific idea of what your career path should look like and be able to express it in a concise and efficient manner.

Don't be afraid to get specific. Do you want to be a director? Say it straight up – "I want to be a director." Be confident and be specific. Be passionate about it. When you get introduced to someone in the industry who has the ability to assist you in your career, you don't want to be caught dead saying something generic like, "I just want to work in the industry." Nobody wants to work with someone who comes off as wishy-washy about their career goals.

People in the entertainment industry are extremely busy and have little time or patience to waste on wannabes, so you must have already invested your time in training before you label yourself with a particular career goal.

There are plenty of events that provide opportunities to network, but not all events are created equal. To make the best use of your time, you must focus on depth over breadth. Your networking activities will be far more productive if you are active in a few organizations than if you merely attend a different event every night.

Of course, you can't plan every encounter or networking opportunity. There are divine appointments that appear as impromptu meetings and chance encounters. You really never know who that guy standing in line in front of you at Starbucks is, or who they know. Sometimes just doing something nice for another person - holding the door for them when their hands are full - can result in a rewarding networking opportunity.

When prepping for a networking event, take an interest in the people you hope to connect with. Try to figure out what they need, how you can help them, and who you know that might benefit from knowing them.

"Whenever I connect people in my own network," Torry says, "I send some biographical background information about the people I am introducing and make suggestions of how I think the introduction can benefit each party."

"Mr. Filmmaker, I want to introduce you to my friend, [insert actor friend's name here] who is a great actor. I think they would work great in that new film you were telling me about."

While you can always network at any event, such as a concert, film festival, or business lunch, you don't have to wait for an event. You can always create one. Consider hosting your own networking event. Schedule a lunch and invite six to eight friends who work in different sectors of the same field. It really doesn't help to have eight actors sitting at the same table, but if you have a couple of actors, a film score pro, a director, a film finance expert and a casting agent at the same table, the possibilities are endless.

Depending on source, up to 75% of all jobs are filled by people on the inside. The bottom line is, people like to work with people they already know. Networking is the primary way you can get to know the movers and shakers. And it is the way you can introduce people you know to people who need their skills.

Where to Network

So, where do you network? Everywhere. The fact is, you are never not networking. But here are a few suggestions when you want to be intentional about it:

Industry Specific Conferences, Festivals and Events - Conferences, festivals and industry events are great places to connect with industry newcomers and established veterans. They are also the primary place where you will discover new trends in the business.

Educational Establishments - Whether you are taking classes to keep current in your industry, or attending your 10 year high school reunion, chances are someone in your class - or who was in your class - has the expertise you need to take your career to the next level. Or they may need your expertise for their next project.

On Set or On Stage - If you are a performing artist, or if you work behind the scenes in the performing arts, your co-workers are some of your best resources. You can make a lot of great contacts by hanging out with the cast and crew after the performance, shoot or rehearsal is over. But also be totally professional while on set. If you are the kind of pro that everyone loves to have on set, chances are the powers that be will want to have you on set again.

Professional Associations - Don't go crazy by joining every organization in town, but it doesn't hurt to be affiliated with one or two professional associations. It looks good on your resume, and you might just find a kindred spirit in that room full of knowledgeable professionals who are also looking to network with each other and with you.

Social Networking - We've already talked about networking on your social media websites. You can also network while you are socializing. We are not, of course, advocating turning your dinner date into an opportunity to sell yourself for a business deal, but chance encounters at a social gathering can be fertile ground for future assignments. Just keep your eyes open for those divine appointments.

Working the Room

Torry insists that you don't have to be an extrovert to work a room and come away with a pocketful of new contacts and improved relationships. Even if you are the shy and reserved type, there are ways to make the most of networking events. These tips will get you into the room and involved in some relaxed chatting in a style that is comfortable for you.

Arrive Early - It's easier to greet people who are arriving than it is to enter a gathering in full swing and find conversations to join. As an early arrival, you can stake out your turf. You can introduce newcomers to one another. You become the go-to guy, rather than the guy standing on the outside looking in.

Approach People - Social gatherings can be awkward if you don't know many of the people who are there. You can easily recognize those people. They are the ones who are standing alone, sipping a soda and not talking to anyone. Wander over and introduce yourself. You never know who you'll meet. Even if this isn't a person you'll want to follow up with, the interaction will get you warmed up.

"I did this at a conference once," Torry recalls, "and after 10 minutes of chatting with a man who was standing alone and leaning against the wall, I finally discover that he was the janitor. He made one of the most important introductions for me, however, as he had a niece who was a casting director which led to a job for me."

Stuff like that just happens to Torry.

Converse - Standing around is boring, awkward and a

complete waste of your networking opportunity. Go ahead. Break the ice. It is as simple as the journalistic standard of *who, what, where when, why.* Just walk up to someone you don't know and say, "Hi, I'm [*insert your name here*]. What's your name? What do you do? [pause and *listen*] Where are you from? [pause and *listen* again] How long have you been in the industry? [and *listen* - this is a conversation, remember?] Why are you here? [We're certain that we don't need to remind you to *listen.*]"

Read the Nametags - There is a reason retail stores and restaurants make their employees wear nametags. Calling someone by their name is just a whole lot more pleasant than saying, 'Hey, you!' If you're not sure how to pronounce a person's name, asking how with a smile and a comment on what a lovely name it is can be a great opening.

Exchange Business Cards - We don't necessarily advocate carrying that brand name credit card, but you should never leave home without your business card. Keep them in a case that is designed for just such a purpose. A sweaty, wrinkled business card is not a great introduction to your professional persona. When you exchange business cards, try to jot a note on the back of the card to remind you of any important information that came up during your conversation. If you spoke to several folks during the evening, they all tend to run together. It's helpful to have some information to jog your memory.

Car PR - Occasionally it will be your turn to drive. You want the people who ride with you to perceive you as a complete pro, and having a floorboard full of candy wrappers and empty soda cans isn't the way to do it. Keep your car neat and clean - or at least clean it before it is your time to drive.

It's NOT All About You - Social gatherings can be anxious and awkward times for anyone who doesn't know everyone at the function. You can alleviate some of that awkwardness by focusing on others from the very beginning. Be interesting *and* interested. If you put your energy into making others feel comfortable, you'll likely find yourself more relaxed as well.

Tips for Successful Networking

Successful networking is a social process, and knowing where to do it is only half of the game. Polish up your social skills and remember, opportunity can and does knock at unusual times.

Don't Be Afraid To Ask for Advice - There are plenty of people in your industry who know more than you do, and many of them are willing and eager to share with up-and-comers. When you meet professionals whose work you admire, don't be afraid to ask for their advice. Don't be pushy and be respectful of their time. You never know if they have a few minutes to talk unless you ask.

Help Others - What goes around, comes around. When you put in a good word for others, they'll remember. At some point in the future, usually when you least expect it, they'll be in a position to return the favor. Remember the biblical story of Joseph and Pharaoh's butler? It's tough enough to make a living in the creative arts. It's good to have allies.

Stay Engaged - Never write off a good contact. Networking is not just about making friends; it's about helping them, keeping up with them, and staying involved with their lives. It takes work. But it's worth it.

Keep Your Promotional Materials Handy - Your promotional materials won't do you any good if you leave them at home. If you carry a brief case, keep a copy of your press kit in it. Have a copy of your demo reel, latest CD, book or DVD in your car. You don't want to hand them out like candy, but all that great networking just falls by the wayside if you don't have immediate access to your work.

The Care and Feeding of Your Network

Making contacts is the first step in networking. Making relationships with those contacts is the time-consuming part.

Contact List - Exchanging business cards at an event is a great first step, but if you stick the card in your wallet and never look at it again you have just wasted your time. As soon as possible, you need to transfer the information on that business card, including any notes you wrote on the back, into your contact list.

Include a note about what you talked about and who introduced you. It wouldn't hurt to send that person an email. You don't need to get creepy about it; just to remind them who you are and to let them know how much you enjoyed making their acquaintance.

Re-connect - Meeting new people is great. Developing relationships is a bit more challenging, but infinitely more rewarding. Of course, you can't fully develop a personal relationship with every person you meet. There is not enough time and you do have other things to do. But if you have the opportunity to reconnect at future gatherings, so much the better. Drop an email and invite them to a book signing or lunch gathering with others. This type of social interaction is non-threatening and creates opportunities for business relationships, as well as friendships, to develop.

Educate Each Other - You can't promote someone else if you don't know what they do. They can't promote you if they don't know your skills. Take the time to understand the goals, desires and abilities of the people your network and make sure they know yours.

Prioritize Your Relationships - Time prevents us from spending extended amounts of time with everyone that we would like to. The same is true with your network. You have to set priorities. You will likely have an inner circle in your network that you go to more often for wisdom and advice. There are people in your network who reciprocate your promotional efforts more than others. Chances are, you will spend more time on those relationships. That's fine and natural, but don't burn any bridges with folks who have not proved to be profitable from a business perspective.

People are still important. You can still have a personal relationship even if you no longer have a useful business relationship. You can and should continue to pray for each other and offer encouragement and support when you can. Of course, you can't stop another person from burning a bridge to you. That hurts when it happens, but the reality is, sometimes it happens.

Networking from a Spiritual Perspective

For us, networking comes under the authority of Christ just like everything else in our lives should. With that in mind, we'd like to share a more spiritual perspective on networking, based on this scripture:

"Do nothing out of selfish ambition or vain conceit; but in humility consider others better than yourself!"

Philippians 2:3

Torry was performing comedy at The Big Stinkin' Comedy Festival in Austin, Texas, when he had the opportunity to sit down and spend an hour with Rick Najera. Rick is a well known producer and writer who was voted one of Hollywood's 50 Most Influential People. He started with Jim Carrey in the TV show "In Living Color."

"We were discussing the power of networking, and Rick shared the _Theory of Building Empires_. According to Rick, his empire is made up of people he has met and worked with; individuals he admired as professionals and enjoyed as people. He takes the same crew and cast from project to project because he prefers working with friends and people he can trust to get the job done," Torry recalls.

Rick is also a part of others people's empires. These entertainment pros built their empires together by going back and forth, helping each other out with their different projects. It is a process that has helped all of them stay continually employed.

"Sometimes you're hot in the entertainment industry and sometimes you're not" Rick told Torry. "That is the ebb and flow of show-biz. It flips back and forth constantly. So whether you're at the top this week or whether one of your friends is, your over-all goal should be to keep working steadily and to do that, staying connected is crucial."

"Rick finished by saying, 'It's important to maintain true friendships with the people you network with, Torry. Remember that. It makes work a lot more fun. After all, I'd much rather work with friends than strangers. Wouldn't you?"'

That conversation changed Torry's life.

"That's where I learned about the concept of building network empires with people I called my friends," Torry explains. "I took that theory and added a spiritual dimension to it. I started thinking of networking not as building an empire for me or for others, but rather as all of us corporately building up the Body of Christ, helping each other to enhance the Kingdom of God together and giving Him the glory. *Empire shmempire*; building God's kingdom is what it's really about. Empires burn and fade away - just ask the Roman's - but God's kingdom, now that's gonna last for eternity."

Holy Introductions - Before every industry event or social gathering, we pray and ask God to direct us to people that we can help, and to direct people to us that can help us; with our mutual goals being to lift up the name of Jesus Christ. Not our name or your name, but *His* name. We also ask for the ability to discern the shiny distractions from the divine appointments. Basically, we ask for "Holy Introductions."

What It Is Not - We're not talking about platform building where it's all about you. We're not talking about the type of social networking where you gather followers or 'friends' by the thousands. While that may be an important aspect of marketing for businesses, filmmakers, authors and recording artists, it has very little for us. In fact, that kind of stuff gets a bit annoying at times.

Think about it; have you ever received several updates

throughout the day from someone announcing every little thing they do?

"Hey, everyone- just had my bangs trimmed!" Then they want you to tell everyone on your social network _i.e. "Dude-go tell EVERYONE that I got my bangs trimmed!!!"_ and then _"Hey! I created a Bang Trimming fan page- if you're a fan of getting your bangs trimmed you should totally join" "Hey-now could you send out an invitation to join my "Bang Trimming" fan page to everyone else on your face book? Thank goodness for bangs! And bang trimmers!!"_

It starts to look more like an advertisement than an update. When we get those types of announcements and invitations from someone on a frequent basis, we turn the other way and run. We're not interested in promoting anyone or anything at the cost of annoying everyone and everything in our network. It's not a wise use of our time and resources. And it is not a wise use of yours either.

What It Is - We network with our friends, people we know - and people we trust - people whose works and character we're familiar with. Because we respect them, we don't want to annoy them by connecting them to someone who is going to disturb them on a regular basis with what amounts to be a personal public relations campaign for someone else.

"I like to think of myself as a match maker really, for the careers of my friends," Torry says. "I'm not married and I don't have kids, so my friends _are_ my kids, figuratively speaking. And just like a parent cares about their children by wanting them to succeed, and by going out of their way to help them, I do the same thing with my friends."

Networking for friends is fun for us. When it works, it's like giving an unexpected gift to someone who truly deserves it. We know that the person we are promoting is trustworthy and truly places expanding God's kingdom as the Number One priority above expanding his own. So in our minds - when we're lifting them up higher, we are lifting Him up higher. We get excited when we see what the Holy Spirit is doing through all the people He is refining and raising up all over this planet. We love connections and relationship and networking, but for us, it must be led by the Spirit or it will all turn to dust and blow away.

Sowing and Reaping - Networking is about offering help and sharing information. It's about being *more* concerned about others than ourselves. It's about loving your neighbor as yourself. When we invest our time and resources in the lives of others we are simply reflecting the scripture about reaping what you sow.

If you sow positive things into the lives of others, you will reap the same in return. It might take years for a connection to pay off. It might not ever pay off in a way you can see. Honestly, not every meeting leads to a connection and not every connection leads to a collaboration. Not all rewards can be seen with the physical eye; *but there is a reward.*

We've worked with people in the Christian entertainment industry who wouldn't share a contact with you if their life depended on it. Sometimes you help someone who then has the ability to help you in return - and they simply won't. Who knows why? Maybe they are afraid of creating their own competition, so they won't make a recommendation or introduction for you, period.

"I once heard a person who had helped someone gain personal success actually express regret for doing so," Torry recalls. "That person turned to me and, with tears in their eyes, said, 'Well, there's another person I helped who passed me by.'"

Why was there bitterness to that? We're supposed to encourage, uplift and rejoice in each other's successes. If there's a person or a way that can bring people closer to God, and if we can be instrumental in making that happen - whether it be from an introduction for that person or a recommendation for a part in a movie that they would be perfect for – we're all for it. Jesus is coming soon, folks. No time for pettiness or this feeling of competition. It's ungodly and divisive.

What About Competition? - It's sad that, even in the Kingdom of God, there are people who feel that by making connections for other people, they are creating their own competition. We should remember that we are not creating competition, but creating opportunities - for others and ourselves. _In that order._

We care about creating opportunities for the expansion of God's kingdom, regardless of who He chooses to use, or how He chooses to use them. We serve a _really big_ God who is fully capable of using all of us. Not just me, and not just you.

Buddy Bags - Instead of worrying about creating competition, consider focusing on creating opportunities for others. This will pay off in the long run in new opportunities for you, either in the natural or spiritual realm. To help him shamelessly promote others, Torry always carries a Buddy Bag in his car.

"I usually have at least 25 business cards each from several of my talented friends that I secure with a rubber band and toss in a canvas bag," Torry explains. "That Buddy Bag goes wherever I go. Then whenever I am presented with an opportunity to promote my friends or make a connection for them, I take that person's business card out of the bag and hand it to the person who can use it. *You need a photographer? Hold on, let me get Allen Clark's business card for you. Need a bio written? Let me get you in touch with Mike Parker or Paula Parker. Need help with a website or branding? Lemme get Kevin Tucker's card.*"

Conditional Networking - If we were the robot on "Lost In Space" we'd be waving our arms and shouting, "Danger, Will Robinson!" There is another type of networker to avoid at all costs. This is the type of person who will indeed make introductions for you, *but* with certain conditions. He wants to be the hub of the wheel and control all the people around him. He wants dictate how they can work together and when they can work together. If any of the people he has connected do work together, well it had better darn well benefit him somehow, or there will be a problem.

This person is a control freak and has the biggest ego in the room. This person wants to take the role of God in all of his network dealings. This kind of networker only has his own self-interests in mind at all times. We have no time for such a person; no respect and no inclination to help or refer people to them. And we don't feel the least bit bad about saying so.

Christians and Chameleons - Believe it or not, even in the field of Christian entertainment people will use you. The will take advantage of you under the guise of friendship, then dump you and take you off their website friends list as soon as you stop benefitting them.

It hurts and we know - we've all been dumped. We'd say don't take it personally, but it's hard not to. It's a shame, but that's life. We're all sinners and fall short. You've got to forgive that person, give them some grace... and move on.

Just because someone says they are a Christian doesn't mean that they have a personal relationship with Jesus. Not everyone's definition of "Christian" lines up with your definition of "Christian." Even the Lord warns us to be as wise as serpents and as harmless as doves.

Some people know key phrases and the right things to say in a Christian environment, but that doesn't mean that they walk the walk. Some people are all things to all people and will compromise their beliefs so as not to offend anyone else and maintain their own popularity. Discernment is a gift of the Spirit; one you need to help you tell the difference between a Christian and a chameleon.

That doesn't mean you refuse to work with them on a professional level. They may be the absolute best at what they do. It does mean you operate your relationship with them purely on a professional level. Expect nothing from them except professional courtesy. Guard your heart and only share it with your trusted friends.

Personal Friends - It's wise to first know the person you are connecting to before connecting them to someone else in you network. [Not doing your proper homework on someone can be a _very_ bad thing and have multiple repercussions.] We're ashamed to admit that there have been a few times that we have been burned by a connection that we didn't properly check out. Either they were not at the level they should be professionally, they weren't who or what they claimed to be, or they weren't as talented as we had hoped. This leads to embarrassment for everyone - the person, ourselves and the person we're connecting them to. Things like that can affect our reputation and cause people to question our judgment, so we're cautious. We advise you to be cautious as well.

"My niece is an actress moving to LA - can you connect them with anyone?"

The answer is 'No.'

We can direct them to workshops and suggest agencies but until we know them personally, we won't risk our reputation by making a recommendation. If we fail someone once, they will always question our judgment in the future. So, while we love to connect others and make holy introductions, we have to know who they are and use godly discernment so we don't waste anyone's time, in order to make the very best connection for each individual. It gets tricky and that's why prayer is so important.

Networking Vs. Social Climbing - There are times where the networking isn't mutual. Sometimes a person will pose as a networker, but she's really just a social climber. It pays to know the difference.

True networking involves ethics. Social climbers just want to see themselves at the top, regardless of who they have to walk on to get there. Let's face it, even in Christian entertainment industry people can get so caught up in their professional success that they forget that they are working for God. When that happens it's easy for people to focus on promoting themselves. There are also a lot of wolves in sheep's clothing in this industry. Use caution and be wise in all your dealings.

Bachelor's Degree From the College of Hard Knocks - Most of the lessons we are sharing with you were learned the hard way. There were times we promoted ourselves and forgot about God. There were times when we compromised in our careers because we had stars – or dollar signs - in our eyes and vain selfish ambitions. We've said and done things that we know have disappointed God.

Conviction isn't always as audible as we'd like it to be because _some_ of us get really good at adjusting the volume on the Holy Spirit. We've been there, done that, bought the T-shirt and earned our diploma from the school of hard knocks. Now, we're trying to live our lives at full volume and without ear muffs because we believe the time is short; that we are in a crucial period of history. We want every day to count. We want more of Him and less of us.

"There was a time when I was tempted to not connect one person in my network to another person in my network because I thought that, by making that connection, it would help another person get ahead and not me," Torry admits. "I was working with a producer and hoping that he'd want one of my screenplays and, in the middle of one of our conversations, he asked if I knew a certain other writer.

"Well, I did indeed know the writer that the producer was inquiring about, but I was hesitant to make the connection because that particular writer wasn't a true networker. I had made several connections for this writer before and he never repaid the favor, and in fact barely even said thank you for any of it. The writer was one of those people who never took the time to network for anyone but himself. It's not that he was a bad guy. He didn't do that intentionally. He was just too wrapped up in his own career to think about helping someone else.

"Soooo...here I was - facing the decision whether to introduce this producer to this writer, knowing full well that by doing so I could potentially be placing the other writer's screenplays in front of this producer rather than my own. I knew that the connection could cost me, so I selfishly decided not to make the connection."

Fortunately, the Holy Spirit isn't one to allow such a situation to go by with consequences.

"For the next 24 hours I was literally *stalked* by the Holy Spirit," Torry confesses. "I was miserable and felt *guilty, guilty, guilty*. There was no escape from it. I talked to my best friend, Rob, about it and he said I was being self-seeking and should make the connection and let God do whatever He wanted with it because there might be a purpose for that producer and writer to be connected.

"Well I didn't like that advice, so I went to my buddy and co-writer, Marshal Younger, and talked to him about it. He said the same thing. *Argh.* I was determined to keep looking until someone said what I wanted to hear so I went to my buddy, Lauren Yarger, next. She said the same thing, too. All three had the same piece of advice. Make the connection. Again, I stubbornly refused. I tossed and turned in bed all night unable to sleep. My brain wouldn't shut off. I then got up and read my Bible, hoping to get some relief and peace and I opened it to the following verse:

"Therefore, to Him Who Knows to Do Good and Does Not Do It, to Him it is Sin." James 4:17 (emphasis ours)

"I knew in that instant what I needed to do," Torry says. "I wasn't particularly happy about it, but there was a huge relief in the decision to connect the two people and the next day, that is exactly what I did. The two then went on to work on a project together that I am certain will expand God's kingdom. And isn't that what it's all about anyway? Expanding God's kingdom?"

We want to encourage you to operate the way the body of Christ is supposed to operate. If you can make a connection within the Body that will benefit the Body, by all means, do it. Even if it doesn't help you. Remember;

"Therefore, to Him Who Knows to Do Good and Does Not Do It, to Him it is Sin." James 4:17. (again, emphasis ours)

Memorize that scripture. You'll save yourself a lot of grief and get a good night's sleep.

We know that some of you reading this book have stars in your eyes and high expectations. You think you know someone who has the ability to help you; that they _should_ and that they _will_ help you. You have high expectations of them.

Don't.

You are going to be crushed and hurt if you come at people with expectation. Having high expectations of God is good. Having high expectations of people... not so much. Don't try to force doors open that God isn't opening. Some people don't want to help. Some people aren't supposed to help. Some people can't help. Chances are even if you have a discerning spirit, you have a hard time figuring out which is which. It's hard to understand and accept that. The best you can do is trust God and let him arrange your path.

It's All About Him - Sometimes it seems easier to have this "good sportsmanship" feeling when you are just starting out and are at the bottom of the totem pole. Sometimes when you are at the top of your game and everything is coming up roses that your perspective shifts and you start viewing everyone else, even brothers and sisters in Christ, as nothing more than competition.

It's kind of like how some folks crowd into church after an earthquake devastates their home, but can't find the time for a worship service when things are going good and there's lots of money in the bank account. We really shouldn't be surprised then when people in this industry treat each other the same way.

Strive to make a difference and you will. Even if the only person who ever changes is you.

Trilogy of Trust - Bill Gates has spoken of a trilogy of trust – the trust that one person has in another, that is then passed on to the third party. For example, Torry knows, likes and trusts Mike, who knows likes and trusts Paula. Based on this two-way trust, Torry will be open to discussions or possible connections with Paula, even though Paula has never previously had contact with Torry. Smart networkers know that a good word spoken about them by one person of influence to another person of influence will carry a lot of weight with that person.

Everybody is a Somebody - Dismissing people because you think they are 'nobodies' is absolute foolishness. Nobody is a nobody. Good networkers know that everyone is connected to others, and that everyone is a somebody, somewhere.

Never Use People - Master networkers never use people. Doing unto others as you would have them do unto you is mandatory if you are to be thought of favorably by the assortment of people you meet in your profession and throughout your life.

Not Everyone Will Like You - It hurts, but it's okay. When you feel the sting of someone not liking you, take a trip to Psalm 37 and spend some time focusing on it. There is lots to think about in that Psalm and "not fretting" is mentioned three times in it - and with good reason.

Be For *Giving* But Don't Forget - Good networkers give without remembering and receive without forgetting.

The Bottom Line - Be professional. Be generous. Think of others first. Pray for holy introductions and God's will. Love others as yourself. Remember, you reap what you sow.

We started out this chapter with the old saying, "It's not what you know but who you know?" And that is true.

The most powerful and important person to know in the universe is God. He is the most important connection you will ever make. Maintain that relationship first. Make it a priority. He's the best networker we know; and that is God's own truth.

Networking - just like anything else - needs to be brought under the lordship of Jesus Christ. Take it there, leave it there and trust Him to empower you and guide you. This chapter is called "The Power of Networking" but we'd really like to think of it as being "Empowered for Networking."

They say that if you truly want people to remember something that you need to say it three times. So here once again is our most emphatic and not-so-gentle all important reminder of what we believe should be the true heart should be for a networking believer.

"Do nothing out of selfish ambition or vain conceit; but in humility consider others better than yourself!"
                                                   Philippians 2:3

Resources

This book could not have been completed without input from a plethora of friends and colleagues.

Rene Gutteridge - author
GP Taylor - author
Allen Clark - photographer
Nancy Stafford - actress/author
Jenn Gotzon - actress
Larry Wayne - radio personality/voice over artist
Melissa Campbell Goodson - public relations
Dennis Disney - public relations
Holly McClure - reviewer/television executive
Kevin & Becky Tucker - marketing executives
Doug Griffin - radio personality
Marshal Younger - screenwriter
Lauren Yarger - Broadway reviewer

Made in the USA
Charleston, SC
03 March 2014